I0534321

HEART

A Social Novel

MARTIN FARQUHAR TUPPER, A.M., F.R.S.

1st WORLD
LIBRARY
Literary Society

Heart

Martin Farquhar Tupper

© 1st World Library, 2007
PO Box 2211
Fairfield, IA 52556
www.1stworldlibrary.com
First Edition

LCCN: 2007930808

Softcover ISBN: 978-1-4218-4851-8
Hardcover ISBN: 978-1-4218-4754-2
eBook ISBN: 978-1-4218-4948-5

Purchase *"Heart"*
as a traditional bound book at:
www.1stWorldLibrary.com/purchase.asp?ISBN=978-1-4218-4851-8

1st World Library is a literary, educational organization
dedicated to:

- Creating a free internet library of downloadable ebooks

- Hosting writing competitions and offering book publishing
  scholarships.

Interested in more 1st World Library books? contact:
literacy@1stworldlibrary.com
Check us out at: www.1stworldlibrary.com

1ˢᵗ World Library Literary Society

Giving Back to the World

"If you want to work on the core problem, it's early school literacy."

- James Barksdale, former CEO of Netscape

"No skill is more crucial to the future of a child, or to a democratic and prosperous society, than literacy."

- Los Angeles Times

"Literacy... means far more than learning how to read and write... The aim is to transmit... knowledge and promote social participation."

- UNESCO

"Literacy is not a luxury, it is a right and a responsibility. If our world is to meet the challenges of the twenty-first century we must harness the energy and creativity of all our citizens."

- President Bill Clinton

"Parents should be encouraged to read to their children, and teachers should be equipped with all available techniques for teaching literacy, so the varying needs and capacities of individual kids can be taken into account."

- Hugh Mackay

CHAPTER I

WHEREIN TWO ANXIOUS PARENTS
HOLD A COLLOQUY

"Is he rich, ma'am? is he rich? ey? what—what? is he rich?"

Sir Thomas was a rapid little man, and quite an epicure in the use of that luscious monosyllable.

"Is he rich, Lady Dillaway? ey? what?"

"Really, Thomas, you never give me time to answer," replied the quintescence of quietude, her ladyship; "and then it is perpetually the same question, and—"

"Well, ma'am, can there be a more important question asked? I repeat it, is he rich? ey? what?

"You know, Sir Thomas, we never are agreed about the meaning of that word; but I should say, very."

As Lady Dillaway always spoke quite softly in a whisper, she had failed to enlighten the knight; but he seemed, notwithstanding, to have caught her intention instinctively; for he added, in his impetuous, imperious way,

"No nonsense now, about talents and virtues, and all such trash; but quick, ma'am, quick—is the man rich?"

"In talents, as you mention the word, certainly, very rich; a more clever or accomplished—"

"Cut it short, ma'am—cut it short, I say—I'll have no adventurers, who live by their wits, making up to my daughter—pedantic puppies, good for ushers, nothing else. What do they mean by knowing so much? ey? what?"

"And then, Sir Thomas, if you will only let me speak, a man of purer morals, finer feelings, higher Christian—"

"Bah! well enough for curates: go on, ma'am—go on, and make haste to the point of all points—is he rich?"

"You know I never will make haste, Thomas, for I never can have patience, and you shall hear; I am little in the habit of judging people entirely by their purses, not even a son-in-law, provided there is a sufficiency on the one side or the other for—"

"Quick, mum—quick—rich—rich? will the woman drive me mad?" and Sir Thomas Dillaway, Knight, rattled loose cash in both pockets more vindictively than ever. But the spouse, nothing hurried, still crept on in her *sotto voce adantino* style.

"Mr. Clements owes nothing, has something, and above and beside all his good heart, good mind, good fame, good looks, good family, possesses a contented—"

"Pish! contented, bah!" our hasty knight's nose actually curled upwards in utter scorn as he added, "Now, that's enough—quite enough. I'll bet a plum the man's poor.

Contented indeed! did you ever know a rich man yet who was contented—ey? mum—ey? or a poor one that wasn't—ey? what? I've no patience with those contented fellows: it's my belief they steal away the happiness of monied men. If this Mr. Clements was rich—rich, one wouldn't mind so much about talents, virtues, and contentment—work-house blessings; but the man's poor, I know it—poo-o-or!"

Sir Thomas had a method quite his own of pronouncing those contradictory monosyllables, rich and poor: the former he gave out with an unctuous, fish-saucy gusto, and the word seemed to linger on his palate as a delicious morsel in the progress of delightful deglutition; but when he uttered the word poor, it was with that "mewling and puking" miserable face, appropriated from time immemorial to the gulping of a black draught.

"No, Lady Dillaway, right about's the next word I shall say to that smooth-looking pauper, Mr. Henry Clements—to think of his impudence, making up to my daughter, indeed! a poo-o-o-r man, too."

"I did not tell you he was poor, Sir Thomas: you have run away with that idea on your own account: the young man has enough for the present, owes nothing for the past, and reasonable expectations for the—

"Future, I suppose, ey? what? I hate futures, all the lot of 'em: cash down, ready money, bird in the hand, that's my ticket, mum: expectations, indeed! Well, go on—go on; I'm as patient as a—as a mule, you see; go on, will you; I may as well hear it all out, Lady Dillaway."

"Well, Sir Thomas, since you think so little of the future, I will not insist on expectations; though I really can only excuse your methods of judging by the fancy that you are far too prudent in fearing for the future: however, if you will not admit this, let me take you on your own ground, the present; perhaps Mr. Clements may not possess quite as much as I could wish him, but then surely, dear Thomas, our daughter must have more than—"

I object to seeing oaths in print; unless it must be once in a way, as a needful point of character: probably the reader's sagacity will supply many omissions of mine in the eloquence of Sir Thomas Dillaway and others. But his calm spouse, nothing daunted, quietly whispered on—"You know, Thomas, you have boasted to me that your capital is doubling every year; penny-postage has made the stationery business most prosperous; and if you were wealthy when the old king knighted you as lord mayor, surely you can spare something handsome now for an only daughter, who—"

"Ma'am!" almost barked the affectionate father, "if Maria marries money, she shall have money, and plenty of it, good girl; but if she will persist in wedding a beggar, she may starve, mum, starve, and all her poverty-stricken brats too, for any pickings they shall get out of my pocket. Ey? what? you pretend to read your Bible, mum—don't you know we're commanded to 'give to him that hath, and to take away from him that—'"

"For shame, Sir Thomas Dillaway!" interrupted the wife, as well she might, for all her quietude: she was a good sort of woman, and her better nature aroused its wrath at this vicious application of a truth so just when applied to morals and graces, so bitterly iniquitous in the case of this world's wealth. I wish that our ex-lord mayor's distorted text may not be one of real and common usage. So, silencing her lord, whose character it was to be overbearing to the meek, but cringing to any thing like rebuke or opposition, she forthwith pushed her advantages, adding—

"Your income is now four thousand a-year, as you have told me, Thomas, every hour of every day, since your last lucky hit in the government contract for blue-elephants and whitey-browns. We have only John and Maria; and John gets enough out of his own stock-brokering business to keep his curricle and belong to clubs—and—alas! my fears are many for my poor dear boy—I often wish, Thomas, that our John was not so well supplied with money: whereas, poor Maria—"

"Tush, ma'am, you're a fool, and have no respect at all for monied men. Jack's a rich man, mum—knows a trick or two, sticks at nothing on 'Change, shrewd fellow, and therefore, of course I don't stint him: ha! he's a regular Witney comforter, that boy—makes money—ay, for all his seeming extravagance, the clever little rogue knows how to keep it, too. If you only knew, ma'am, if you only knew—but we don't blab to fools."

I dare say "fools" will hear the wise man's secret some day.

"Well, Thomas, I am sure I have no wish to pry into business transactions; all my present hope is to help the cause of our poor dear Maria."

"Don't call the girl 'poor,' Lady Dillaway; it's no recommen-dation, I can tell you, though it may be true enough. Girls are a bad spec, unless they marry money. If our girl does this, well; she will indeed be to me a dear Maria, though not a poo-o-o-r one; if she doesn't, let her bide, and be an old maid; for as to marrying this fellow Clement's, I'll cut him adrift to-morrow."

"If you do, Sir Thomas, you will break our dear child's heart."

"Heart, ma'am! what business has my daughter with a heart?" [what, indeed?] "I hate hearts; they were sent, I believe, purposely to make those who are plagued with 'em poo-o-o-r. Heart, indeed! When did heart ever gain money? ey? what? It'll give, O yes, plenty—plenty, to charities, and churches, and orphans, and beggars, and any thing else, by way of getting rid of gold; but as to gaining—bah! heart indeed—pauperizing bit of muscle! save me from wearing under my waistcoat what you're pleased to call a heart. No, mum, no; if the girl has got a heart to break, I've done with her. Heart indeed! she either marries money and my blessing, or marries beggary and my curse. But I should like to know who wants her to marry at all? Let her die an old maid."

Probably this dialogue need go no farther: in the coming chapter we will try to be didactic. Meantime, to apostrophize ten words upon that last heartless sentence:

"Let her die an old maid." An old maid! how many unrecorded sorrows, how much of cruel disappointment and heart-cankering delay, how often-times unwritten tragedies are hidden in that thoughtless little phrase! O, the mass of blighted hopes, of slighted affections, of cold neglect, and foolish contumely, wrapped up in those three syllables! Kind heart, kind heart, never use them; neither lightly as in scorn, nor sadly as in pity: spare that ungenerous reproach. What! canst thou think that from a feminine breast the lover, the wife, the mother, can be utterly sponged away without long years of bitterness? Can Nature's wounds be cicatrized, or her soft feelings seared, without a thousand secret pangs? Hath it been no trial to see youthful bloom departing, and middle age creep on, without some intimate one to share the solitude of life? Ay, and the coming prospect too—hath it greater consolations than the retrospect? How faintly common friends can fill that hollow of the heart! How feebly can their kindness, at the warmest, imitate the sympathies and love of married life! And in the days of sickness, or the hour of death—to be lonely, childless, husbandless, to be lightly cared for, little missed—who can wonder that all those bruised and broken yearnings should ferment within the solitary mind, and some, times sour up the milk of human kindness? Be more considerate, more just, more loving to that injured heart of woman; it hath loved deeply in its day; but imperative duty or untoward circumstances nipped those early blossoms, and often generosity towards others, or the constancy of youthful blighted love, has made it thus alone. There was an age in this world's history, and may be yet again (if Heart is ever to be monarch of this social sphere), when those who lived and died as Jephthah's daughter, were reckoned worthily with saints and martyrs; Heed thou, thus, of many such, for they have offered up their hundred warm yearnings, a hecatomb of human love, to God, the betrothed of their affections; and they move up and down among this inconsiderate world, doing good, Sisters of Charity, full of pure benevolence, and beneficent beyond the widow's mite. Heed kinder then, and blush for very shame, O man and woman! looking on this noble band of ill-requited virgins; remember all their trials, and imitate their deeds; for among the legion of that unreguarded sisterhood whom you coldly call old maids, are often seen the world's chief almoners of warm unselfish sympathy, generous in mind, if not in means, and blooming with the immortal youth of charity and kindliness.

CHAPTER II

HOW THE DAUGHTER HAS A HEART;
AND, WHAT IS COMMONER, A LOVER

Yes, Maria Dillaway, though Sir Thomas's own daughter, had a heart, a warm and good one: it was her only beauty, but assuredly at once the best adornment and cosmetic in the world. The mixture of two such conflicting characters as her father and mother might (with common Providence to bless the pair) unitedly produce heart; although their plebeian countenances could hardly be expected without a direct miracle to generate beauty. Maria inherited from her father at once his impetuosity and his little button-nose: although the latter was neither purple nor pimply, and the former was more generous and better directed: from her mother she derived what looked to any one at first sight very like red hair, along with great natural sweetness of disposition: albeit her locks had less of fire, and her sweetness more of it: sympathy was added to gentleness, zeal to patience, and universal tenderness to a general peace with all the world; for that extreme quietude, almost apathy, alluded to before, having been superseded by paternal impetuosity, the result of all was Heart. She doated on her mother; and (how she contrived this, it is not quite so easy to comprehend) she found a great deal loveable even in her father. But in fact she loved every body. Charity was the natural atmosphere of her

Martin Farquhar Tupper

kind and feeling soul—always excusing, assisting, comforting, blessing; charity lent music to her tongue, and added beauty to her eyes—charity gave grace to an otherwise ordinary figure, and lit her freckled cheek with the spirit of loveliness. Let us be just—nay, more: let us be partial, to the good looks of poor dear Maria. Notwithstanding the snub nose (it is not snub; who says it is snub?—it is *mignon*, personified good nature)—notwithstanding the carroty hair (I declare, it was nothing but a fine pale auburn after all)—notwithstanding the peppered face (oh, how sweetly rayed with smiles!) and the common figure (gentle, unobtrusive, full of delicate attentions)—yes, notwithstanding all these unheroinals, no one who had a heart himself could look upon Maria without pleasure and approval. She was the very incarnation of cheerfulness, kindness, and love: you forgot the greenish colour of those eyes which looked so tenderly at you, and so often-times were dimmed with tears of unaffected pity; her smile, at any rate, was most enchanting, the very sunshine of an amiable mind; her lips dropped blessings; her brow was an open plain of frankness and candour; sincerity, warmth, disinterested sweet affections threw such a lustre of loveliness over her form, as well might fascinate the mind alive to spiritual beauty: and altogether, in spite of natural defects and disadvantages—*nez retroussé*, Cleopatra locks, and all—no one but those constituted like her materialized father and his kind, ever looked upon Maria without unconsciously admiring her, he scarcely knew for what. Though there appeared little to praise, there certainly was every thing to please; and faulty as in all pictorial probability was each lineament of face and line of form, taken separately and by detail, the veil of universal charity softened and united them into one harmonious whole, making of Maria Dillaway a most pleasant, comfortable, wife-like little personage.

At least, so thought Henry Clements. Neither was it any

sudden fortnight's fancy, but the calm consideration of two full years. Maria's was a character which grew upon your admiration gradually—a character to like at first just a little; then to be led onwards imperceptibly from liking to loving; and thence from fervid summer probably to fever heat. She dawned upon young Henry like the blush of earliest morn, still shining brighter and fairer till glorious day was come.

He had casually made her acquaintance in the common social circle, and even on first introduction had been much pleased, not to say captivated, with her cordial address, frank unsophisticated manners, and winsome looks; he contrasted her to much advantage with the affected coquette, the cold formal prude, the flippant woman of fashion, the empty heads and hollow hearts wherewithal society is peopled. He had long been wearied out with shallow courtesies, frigid compliments, and other conventional hypocrisies, up and down the world; and wanted something better to love than mere surface beauty, mere elegant accomplishment—in a word, he yearned for Heart, and found the object of his longings in affectionate Maria.

This first casual acquaintance he had of course taken every opportunity to improve as best he might, and happily found himself more and more charmed on every fresh occasion. How heartily glad she was to see him! how unaffectedly sincere in her amiable joy! how like a kind sister, a sympathizing friend, a very true-love—a dear, cheerful, warm-hearted girl, who would make the very model for a wife!

It is little wonder that, with all external drawbacks, now well-nigh forgotten, the handsome Henry Clements found her so attractive; nor that, following diligently his points of advantage, he progressed from acquaintanceship to intimacy, and intimacy to avowed admiration; and thence (between ourselves) to the resolute measure of engagement.

I say between ourselves, because nobody else in the world knew it but the billing pair of lovers; and even they have got the start of us only by a few hours. As for Henry Clements, he was a free man in all senses, with nobody to bias his will or control his affections—an orphan, unclogged by so much as an uncle or aunt to take him to task on the score of his attachment, or to plague him with impertinent advice. His father, Captain Clements of the seventieth, had fallen "gloriously" on the bloody field of Waterloo, and the pensioned widow had survived her gallant hero barely nine winters; leaving little Henry thrown upon the wide world at ten years of age, under the nominal guardianship of some very distant Ulster cousin of her own, a Mackintosh, Mackenzie, or Macfarlane—it is not yet material which; and as for the lad's little property, his poor patrimony of two hundred a-year had hitherto amply sufficed for Harrow and for Cambridge (where he had distinguished himself highly), for his chambers in the Temple, and his quiet bachelor-mode of life as a man of six-and-twenty.

Accordingly, our lover took counsel of nobody but Maria's beaming eyes, when he almost unconsciously determined to lay siege to her: he really could not make up his mind to the preliminary formal process of storming Sir Thomas in his counting-house, at the least until he had made sure that Maria's kind looks were any thing more particular than universal charity; and as to Lady Dillaway, it was impossible to broach so delicate a business to her till the daughter had looked favourably as aforesaid, set aside her ladyship's formidable state of quiescence, and apparent (though only apparent) lack of sympathy. So the lover still went on sunning his soul from time to time in Maria's kindly smiles, until one day, that is, yesterday, they mutually found out by some happy accident how very dear they were to each other;

and mutually vowed ever to continue so. It was quite a surprise this, even to both of them—an extemporary unrehearsed outburst of the heart; and Maria discovered herself pledged before she had made direct application to mamma about the business. However, once done, she hastened to confide the secret to her mother's ear, earnestly requesting her to break it to papa. With how little of success, we have learnt already.

CHAPTER III

PATERNAL AMIABILITIES

Maria, as we know, loved her father, for she loved every thing that breathes; but she would not have been human had she not also feared him. In fact, he was to her a very formidable personage, and one would have thought any thing but an amiable one. Over Maria's gentle kindness he could domineer as loftily as he would cringe in cowardly humiliation to the boisterous effrontery of that unscrupulous and wily stock-jobber, "my son Jack." With the tyranny proper to a little mind, he would trample on the neck of a poor meek daughter's filial duty, desiring to honour its parent by submission; and then, with consistent meanness, would lick the dust like a slave before an undutiful only son, who had amply redeemed all possible criminalities by successful (I did not say honest) gambling in the funds, and otherwise.

Yes! John Dillaway was rich; and, climax to his praise, rich by his own keen skill, independent of his father, though he condescended still to bleed him. In this "money century," as Kohl, the graphic traveller, has called it, riches "cover the multitude of sins;" leaving poor Maria's charity to cover its own naked virtues, if it can. So John was the father's darling, notwithstanding the very heartless and unbecoming conduct he had exhibited daily for these thirty years, and the marked scorn wherewithal he treated that pudgy city knight, his dear progenitor; but then, let us repeat it as Sir Thomas did—Jack was rich—rich, and such a comfort to his father; whereas Maria, poor fool, with all her cheap unmarketable love and duty, never had earned a penny—never could, but was born to be a drain upon him. Therefore did he scorn her, and put aside her kindnesses, because she could not "make money."

For what end on earth should a man make money! It is reasonable to reply, for the happiness' sake of others and himself; but, in the frequent case of a rich and cold Sir Thomas, what can be the object in such? Not to purchase happiness therewith himself, nor yet to distribute it to others; a very dog in the manger, he snarls above the hay he cannot eat, and is full of any thoughts rather than of giving: whilst, as for his own pleasure, he manifestly will not stop a minute to enjoy a taste of happiness, even if he finds it in his home; nay, more, if it meets him by the way, and wishes to cling about his heart, he will be found often to fling it off with scorn, as a reaper would the wild sweet corn-flower in some handful of wheat he is cutting. O, Sir Thomas! is not poor Maria's love worth more than all your rich rude Jack's sudden flush of money? is it not a deeper, higher, purer, wiser, more abundant source of pleasure? You have yet to learn the wealth of her affections, and his poverty of soul.

It was not without heart-sickness, believe me, sore days and weeping nights, that affectionate Maria saw her father growing more and more estranged from her. True, he had never met her love so warmly that it was not somewhat checked and chilled; true, his nature had reversed the law of reason, by having systematically treated her with less and less of kindness ever since the nursery; she did seem able to remember something like affection in him while she was a prattling infant; but as the mental daylight dawned apace, and she grew (one would fancy) worthier of a rational creature's love, it strangely had diminished year by year; moreover, she could scarcely look back upon one solitary occasion, whereon her father's voice had instructed her in knowledge, spoken to her in sympathy, or guided her footsteps to religion. Still, habituated as she long had now become to this daily martyrdom of heart, and sorely bruised by coarse and common worldliness as had been every fibre of her feelings, she could not help perceiving that things got worse and worse, as the knight grew richer and richer; and often-times her eyes ran over bitterly for coldness and neglect. There was, indeed, her mother to fly to; but she never had been otherwise than a very quiet creature, who made but little show of what feeling she possessed; and then the daughter's loving heart was affectionately jealous of her father too.

"Why should he be so cold, with all his impetuosity? so formal, in spite of his rapidity? so little generous of spirit, notwithstanding all his wonderful prosperity?"

Ah, Maria, if you had not been quite so unsophisticated, you would have left out the latter "notwithstanding." Nothing hardens the heart, dear child, like prosperity; and nothing dries up the affections more effectually than this hot pursuit of wealth. The deeper a man digs into the gold mine, the less able—ay, less willing—is he to breathe the sweet air of upper earth, or to bask in the daylight of heaven: downward, downward still, he casts the anchor of his grovelling affections, and neither can nor will have a heart for any thing but gold.

Moreover, have you wondered, dear Maria, at the common fact (one sees it in every street, in every village), that parental love is oftenest at its zenith in the nursery, and then falls lower and lower on the firmament of human life, as the child gets older and older? Look at all dumb brutes, the lower animals of this our earth; is it not thus by nature's law with them? The lioness will perish to preserve that very whelp, whom she will rend a year or two hence, meeting the young lion in the forest; the hen, so careful of her callow brood, will peck at them, and buffet them away, directly they are fully fledged; the cow forgets how much she once loved yonder well-grown heifer; and the terrier-bitch fights for a bit of gristle with her own two-year-old, whom she used to nurse so tenderly, and famished her own bowels to feed. And can you expect that men, who make as little use as possible of Heart, that unlucrative commodity—who only exercise Reason for shrewd purposes of gain, not wise purposes of good, and who might as well belong to Cunningham's "City of O," for any souls they seem to carry about with them— can you expect that such unaffectioned, unintelligent, unspiritualized animals, can rise far above the brute in feeling for their offspring? No, Maria; the nursery plaything grows into the exiled school-boy; and the poor child, weaned from all he ought to love, soon comes to be regarded in the light of an expensive youth; he is kept at arm's length, unblest, uncaressed, unloved, unknown; then he grows up apace, and tops his father's inches; he is a man now, and may well be turned adrift; if he can manage to make money, they are friends; but if he can only contrive to spend it, enemies. Then the complacent father moans about ingratitude, for he did his duty by the boy in sending him to school.

O, faults and follies of the by-gone times, which lingered even to a generation now speedily passing away!—ye are waning with it, and a better dawn has broken on the world. Happily for man, the multiplication of his kind, and pervading competition in all manner, of things mercantile, are breaking down monopolies, and hindering unjust accumulation, with its necessary love of gain. "Satisfied with little" is young England's cry; a better motto than the "Craving after much" of their fathers. No longer immersed, single-handed, in a worldly business, which seven competitors now relieve him of; no longer engrossed with the mint of gold gains, which a dozen honest rivals now are sharing with him eagerly, the parent has leisure to instruct his children's minds, to take an interest in their pursuits, and to cultivate their best affections. Home is no longer the place perpetually to be driven from; the voices of paternal duty and domestic love are thrillingly raised to lead the tuneful chorus of society; and fathers, as well as mothers, are beginning to desire that their children may be able to remember them hereafter as the ever-sympathizing friend, the wisely indulgent teacher, the guide of their religion, and the guardian of their love; quite as much as the payer of their bills and the filler of their purses.

The misfortune of a past and passing generation has been, too much money in too few hands; its faults, neglect of duty; its folly, to expect therefrom the too-high meed of well-earned gratitude; and from this triple root has grown up social selfishness, a general lack of Heart. No parent ever yet, since the world was, did his duty properly, as God intended him to do it, by the affections of the mind and the yearnings of the heart, as well as by the welfare of the body with its means, and lived to complain of an ungrateful child. He may think he did his duty; oh yes, good easy man! and say so too, very, very bitterly; and the world may echo his most partial verdict, crying shame on the unnatural Goneril and Regan, bad daughters who despise the Lear in old age, or on the dissolute and graceless youth, whose education cost so much, and yields so very little. But money cannot compensate that maiden or that youth for early and habitual injustice done to their budding minds, their sensitive hearts, their craving souls, in higher, deeper, holier things than even cash could buy. "Home affections"—this was the magic phrase inscribed upon the talisman they stole from that graceless youth; and the loss of home affections is scantily counterbalanced at the best by a critical acquaintance with *'Dawes's Canons,'* and *'Bos on Ellipses,'* in his ardent spring of life, and by a little more of the paternal earnings which the legacy-office gives him in his manhood.

But let us not condemn generations past and passing, and wink at our own-time sins; we have many motes yet in our eyes, not to call them very beams. The infant school, the factory, the Union, and other wholesale centralizations, ruin the affections of our poor. O, for the spinning-wheel again within the homely cottage, and those difficult spellings by the grand-dame's knee! There is wisdom and stability in a land thick-set with such early local anchorages; but the other is all false, republican, and unaffectioned. So, too, the luxurious city club has cheated many a young pair of their just domestic happiness, for the husband grew dissatisfied with home and all its poor humilities; whilst a bad political philosophy, discouraging marriage and denouncing off-spring, has insidiously crept into the very core of private families, setting children against parents and parents against children, because a cold expediency winks at the decay of morals, and all united social influences strike at the sacrifice of Heart.

We are forgetting you, poor affectionate Maria, and yet will it comfort your charity to listen. For the time is coming— yea, now is—when a more generous, though poorer age will condemn the Mammon phrensy of that which has preceded it. Boldly do we push our standards in advance, pressing on the flying foe, certain that a gallant band will follow. Fearlessly, here and there, is heard the voice of some solitary zealot, some isolated missionary for love, and truth, and philanthropic good, some dauntless apostle in the cause of Heart, denouncing selfish wealth as the canker of society: and, hark! that voice is not alone; there is a murmur on the breeze as the sound of many waters; it comes, it comes! and the young have caught it up; and manhood hears the thrilling strain that sinks into his soul; and old age, feebly listening, wonders (never too late) that he had not hitherto been wiser; and the whole social universe electrically touched from man to man, I hear them in their new-born generosities, penitently shouting "God and Heart!" even louder than they execrate the memory of Dagon.

CHAPTER IV

EXCUSATORY

It really may be numbered among doubts whether it is possible to exaggerate the dangers into which a fictionist may fall. My marvel is, that any go unstabbed. How on earth did Cervantes continue to grow old, after having pointed the finger of derision at all grave Spain? There is Boccaccio, too; he lived to turn threescore, in spite of the thousand husbands and wives, who might pretty well imagine that he spoke of them. Only consider how many villains, drawn to the life, Walter Scott created. What! were there no heads found to fit his many caps, hats, helmets, and other capillary properties? What! are we so blind, so few of friends, that we cannot each pick out of our social circles Mrs. Gore's Dowager, Mrs. Grey's Flirt, Mrs. Trollope's Widow, and Boz's Mrs. Nickleby? Who can help thinking of his lawyer, when he makes acquaintance with those immortal firms Dodson and Fogg, or Quirk, Snap, and Gammon? Is not Wrexhill libellous, and Dr. Hookwell personal? Arise! avenge them both, ye zealous congregations! Why slumber pistols that, should damage Bulwer? Why are the clasp-knives sheathed, which should have drunk the blood of James? Hath every "[dash] good-natured friend" forgotten to be officious, and neglected to demonstrate to relations and acquaintances that this white villain is Mr. A., and that old virgin poor Miss B.?

Martin Farquhar Tupper

Speak, Plumer Ward, courageous veteran, Have the critics yet forgiven Mr. John Paragraph—forgotten, is impossible? and how is it no house-keeper has arseniicked my soup, O rash recruit, for the mysteries of perquisite divulged in Mrs. Quarles?

A dangerous craft is the tale-wright's, and difficult as dangerous. Human nature goes in casts, as garden-pots do. Lo, you! the crowd of thumb-pots; mean little tiny minds in multitudes, as near alike as possible. Then there are the frequent thirty-twos, average "clever creatures" in this mental age, wherein no one can make an ordinary how-d'ye-do acquaintance without being advertised of his or her surprising talents: and to pass by all intermediate sizes, here and there standing by himself, in all the prickly pride of an immortal aloe, some one big pot monopolizes all the cast of earth, domineering over the conservatory as Brutus's colossal Caesar, or his metempsychosis in a Wellington.

Again: no painter ever yet drew life-likeness, who had not the living models at least in his mind's eye: but no good painter ever yet betrayed the model in his figure; unless (though these instances are rarish too) we except, *pace* Lawrence, the mystery of portraiture. He takes indeed a line here and a colour there; but he softens this and heightens that; so that none but he can well discover any trace of Homer's noble head in yonder sightless beggar, or Juno's queenly form in the Welsh woman trudging with her strawberry load to Covent Garden market.

Flatter not thyself, fair Helen, I have not pictured thee in gentle Grace: tremble not, my little white friend Clatter, thou art by no means Simon Jennings. Dark Caroline Blunt, it is true thou hast fine eyes; nevertheless, in nothing else (I am sorry to assure thee) art thou at all like Emily Warren. Flaunting Lady Busbury, be calm; if you had not been so wrathful, I never should have thought of you—undoubtedly you are not the type of Mrs. Tracy.

Why will all these people don my imaginary characters? Truly, it may seem to be a compliment, as proving that they speak from heart to heart, of universal human nature, not unaptly; still is their inventor or creator embarrassed terribly by such unwelcome honours; your precious balms oppress him, gentle friends; lift off your palm branches; indeed, he is unworthy of these petty triumphs; and, to be serious, he detests them.

No: once and for all, let a plain first person say it, I abjure personalities; my arrows are shot at a venture; and if they hit any one at all, it is only that he stands in my shaft's way, and the harness of his conscience is unbuckled. The target of my feeble aim is general—to pierce the heart of evil, evil in the form of social heartlessness: it is no fault of mine, if some alarmed particulars will crowd about the mark. Ideal characters, ideal incidents, ideal scenes—to these I honestly pledge myself: but as most men have two eyes, being neither naturally monocular nor triocular, so most men of their own special cast have similar distinguishable sympathies.

The overweening love of money is a seed, a soil, and a sun that generates a certain crop: the aim of my poor husbandry is only to reap this; but my sickle does not wish to wound the growers: let them stand aside; or, better far, let them help me cut those rank and clogging tares, and bind them up in bundles to be burned. Heart is a sweet-smelling shrub, ill to stand against the chilling breath of worldliness: my small care desires to cherish this; gather round it, friends! shelter it beside me. How many fragrant flowers now are bursting into beauty! how cheering is their scent! how healthful the aroma of their bloom! Pluck them with me; they are sweet, delicate, and lustrous to look upon, even as the night-blowing cereus.

Martin Farquhar Tupper

Henceforth then, social circle, feel at peace with such as I am, whose public parable would teach, without any thought of personality, entirely disclaiming private interpretations: there are other people stout besides one's uncle, other people deaf besides one's aunt. Sir Thomas Dillaway is not Alderman Bunce, nor any other friend or foe I wot of; a mere creature of the counting-house, he is a human ledger-mushroom: rub away the mildew from your hearts, if any seem to see yourselves in him: neither have I ventured to transplant Miss Cassiopeia Curtis's red hair to dear Maria's head: imitate her graces, if you will, maiden; but charge me not with copying your locks. Though "my son Jack" be a boisterous big rogue, on 'Change, and off it—let not mine own honest stock-broker put that hat upon his head, in the mono-mania that it fits him, because he may heretofore have been both bull and bear; and as for any other heroes yet to come upon this scene, to enact the tragedy or comedy of Heart—"Know all men by these presents,"—your humble servant's will is to smite bad principles, not offending persons; to crusade against evil manners, not his guilty fellow-men.

Wo is me! who am I, that I should satirize my brethren?— Yet, wo is me—if I silently hide the sin I see. Make me not an offender for a word, seeing that my purposes are good. Be not hypercritical, for Heart's sake, against a man whose aim it is to help the cause of Heart. Neither count it sufficient to answer me with an inconclusive "*tu quoque:*" I know it, I feel it, I confess it, I would away with it. Heaven send to him that writes, as liberally as to those who read (yea, more, according to his deeper needs and failings) the grace to counteract all mammonizing blights, and to cultivate this garden of the Heart.

CHAPTER V

WHEREIN A WELL-MEANING MOTHER ACTS VERY FOOLISHLY

Returned from her unsuccessful embassage, Lady Dillaway determined—kind, calm soul—to hide the bitter truth from poor Maria, that her father was inexorably adverse. A scene was of all things that indentical article least liked by the quiescent mother; and that her warm-hearted daughter would enact one, if she heard those echoes of paternal love, was clearly a problem requiring no demonstration.

Accordingly, with well-intentioned kindliness, but shallo-wish wisdom, and most questionable propriety, Maria was persuaded to believe that her father had hem'd and haw'd a little, had objected no doubt to Henry's lack of money, but would certainly, on second thoughts, consider the affair more favourably:

"You know your father's way, my love; leave him to himself, and I am sure his better feeling will not fail to plead your cause: it will be prudent, however, just for quiet's sake, to see less of Henry Clements for a day or two, till the novelty of my intelligence blows over. Meantime, do not cry, dear child; take courage, all will be well; and I will give you my free leave to console your Henry too."

"Dearest, dearest mamma, how can I thank you sufficiently for all this? But why may I not now at once fly to papa, tell him all I feel and wish cordially and openly, and touch his dear kind heart? I am sure he would give us both his sanction and his blessing, if he only knew how much I love him, and my own dear Henry."

"Sweet child," sighed out mamma, "I wish he would, I trust he would, I believe indeed he will some day: but be advised by me, Maria, I know your father better than you do; only keep quiet, and all will come round well. Do not broach the subject to him—be still, quite still; and, above all, be careful that your father does not yet awhile meet Mr. Clements."

"But, dearest mamma, how can I be so silent when my heart is full? and then I hate that gloomy sort of secresy. Do let me ask papa, and tell him all myself. Perhaps he himself will kindly break the ice for me, now that your dear mouth has told him all, mamma. How I wish he would!"

"Alas, Maria, you always are so sanguine: your father is not very much given, I fear, to that sort of sociality. No, my love; if you only will be ruled by me, and will do as I do, managing to hold your tongue, I think you need not apprehend many conversational advances on your father's part."

Poor Maria had more than one reason to fear all this was true, too true; so her lip only quivered, and her eyes overflowed as usual.

Thereafter, Lady Dillaway had all the talk to herself, and she smoothly whispered on without let or hindrance; and what between really hoping things kindly of her husband's better feelings, and desiring to lighten the anxieties of dear Maria's heart, she placed the whole affair in such a calm, warm, and glowing Claude-light, as apparently to supply an emendation (no doubt the right reading) to the well known aphorism—

"The course of true love never did run smooth-*er*."

In fine, our warm and confiding Maria ran up to her own room quite elated after that interview; and she heartily thanked God that those dreaded obstacles to her affection were so easily got over, and that her dear, dear father had proved so kind.

It is quite a work of supererogation to report how speedily the welcome news were made known, by *billet-doux*, to Henry Clements; but they rather smote his conscience, too, when he reflected that he had not yet made formal petition to the powers on his own account. To be sure, they (the lovers, to wit) were engaged only yesterday, quite in an unintended, though delightful, way: and, previously to that important *tête-à-tête*, however much he may have thought of only dear Maria—however frequently he found himself beside her in the circle of their many mutual friends—however happily he hoped for her love—however foolishly he reveried about her kindness in the solitude of his Temple garret—still he never yet had seen occasion to screw his courage to the sticking point, and boldly place his bliss at hard Sir Thomas's disposal. Some day—not yet—perhaps next week, at any rate not exactly to-day—these were his natural excuses; and they availed him even to the other side of that social Rubicon, engagement. Nevertheless, now at length something must decidedly be done; and, within half an hour, Finsbury's deserted square echoed to the heroic knock of Mr. Henry Clements, fully determined upon claiming his Maria at her father's hands.

The knight was out; probably, or rather certainly, not yet returned from his counting-house in St. Benet's Sherehog.

Martin Farquhar Tupper

So, perforce, our hero could only have an audience with his lady.

The same glossing over of unpalatable truths—the same quiet-breathing counsel—the same tranquil sort of hopeful-ness—fully satisfied the lover that his cause was gained. How could he think otherwise? In the father's absence, he had broached that mighty topic to the mother, who even now hailed him as her son, and promised him his father's favour. What could be more delicious than all this? and what more honourable, while prudent, too, and filial, than to acquiesce in Lady Dillaway's fears about her husband's nervousness at the sight of one who was to take from him an only and beloved daughter? It was delicacy itself—charming; and Henry determined to make his presence, for the first few days, as scarce as possible in the sight of that affectionate father.

And thus it came to pass that two open and most honourable minds, pledged to heartiest love, could not find one speck of sin in loving on clandestinely. Nay, was it clandestine at all? Is it, then, merely a legal fiction, and not a religious truth, that husband and wife are one? and is it not quite as much a matrimonial as a moral one that father and mother are so too? Was it not decidedly enough to have spoken to the latter, especially when she undertook to answer for the former? Sir Thomas was a man engrossed in business; and, doubtless, left such affairs of the Heart to the kinder keeping of Lady Dillaway. No; there was nothing secret nor clandestine in the matter; and I entirely absolve both Henry and Maria. They could not well have acted otherwise if any harm should come to it, the mother is to blame.

Lady Dillaway, without doubt, should have known her husband better; but her tranquil love of our dear Maria seemed to have infatuated her into simply believing—what she so much wished—her happiness secure. She heeded not how little sympathy Sir Thomas felt with lovers; and only encouraged her innocent child to play the dangerous game of unconscious disobedience. Accordingly, consistent with that same quiet kindness of character which had smoothed away all difficulties hitherto, the indulgent mother now allowed the loving pair to meet alone, for the first time permissively, to tell each other all their happiness. Lady Dillaway left the drawing-room, and sent Maria to the heart that beat with hers.

Who shall describe the beauty of that interview—the gush of first affections bursting up unchecked, unchidden, as hot springs round the Hecla of this icy world! They loved and were beloved—openly, devotedly, sincerely, disinterestedly. Henry had never calculated even once how much the city knight could give his daughter; and as for Maria, if she had not naturally been a girl all heart, the home wherein she was brought up had so disgusted her of still-repeated riches, that (it is easy of belief) the very name of poverty would be music to her ears. Accordingly, how they flew into each other's arms, and shed many happy tears, and kissed many kindest kisses, and looked many tenderest things, and said many loving words, "let Petrarch's spirit in heroics sing:" as for our present prosaical Muse, she delights in such affections too naturally and simply to wish to cripple them with rhymes, or confine them in sonnets; she despises decoration of simple and beautiful Nature—gilding gold, and painting lilies; and she loves to throw a veil of secret sanctity over all such heaven-blest attachments. "Hence! ye profane," —these are no common lovers: I believe their spirits, still united in affections that increase with time, will go down to the valley of death unchangeably together; and will thence emerge to brighter bliss hand in hand throughout eternity—a double Heart with one pulse, loving God, and good, and one another!

CHAPTER VI

PLEASANT BROTHER JOHN

"Ho, ho! I suspected as much; so this fellow Clements has been hanging about us at parties, and dropping in here so often, for the sake of Miss Maria, ey?"—For the door had noisily burst open to let in Mr. John Dillaway, who under grumbled as above.

"Dear John, I am so rejoiced to see you; I am sure it will make you as happy as myself, brother, to hear the good news: papa and mamma are so kind, and—I need not introduce to you my—you have often met him here, John—Mr. Henry Clements."

"Sir, your most obedient." The vulgar little purse-proud citizen made an impudent sort of distant bow, and looked for all the world like a coated Caliban sarcastically cringing to a well-bred Ferdinand.

Poor Henry felt quite taken aback at such frigid formality; and dear Maria's very heart was in her mouth: but the brother tartly added, "If Mr. Clements wishes to see Sir Thomas—that's his knock: he was following me close behind: I saw him; but, as I make it a point never to walk with the governor, perhaps it's as well for you two I dropped in first by way of notice, ey?"

It was a dilemma, certainly—after all that Lady Dillaway had said and recommended: fortunately, however, her lord the knight, when the street door was opened to him, hastened straightway to his own "study," where he had to consult some treatise upon tare and tret, and a recent pamphlet upon the undoubted social duty, '*Run for Gold*;' so that awkward rencounter was avoided; and Mr. Clements, taking up his hat, was enabled to accomplish a dignified retreat.

"Dear John, your manner grieves me; I wish you had been kinder to my—to Henry Clements."

"Oh, you do, do you? does the governor know of all this? the fellow's a beggar."

"For shame, John! you shall not call my noble Henry such names: of course papa has heard all."

"And approves of all this spooneying, ey, miss?"

"Brother, brother, do be gentler with me: mamma's great kindness has smoothed away all objections, and surely you will be glad, John, to have at last a brother of your own to love you as I do."

"Ey? what? another thief to go shares with me when the governor cuts up? Thank you, miss, I'd rather be excused. You are quite enough, I can tell you, for you make my whole a half; nobody wants a third: much obliged to you, though." [Interjections may as well be understood.]

"O, dear brother, you hurt me, indeed you do: I am sure (if it were right to say so) I would not wish to live a minute, if poor Maria's death could—could make you any happier;—O

John, my heart will—" [Her tears can as readily be understood as his interjections.]

If a domestic railroad could have been cleverly constructed to Maria's chamber from every room in that great house, it would have stood her in good stead; for every day, from some room or other, this poor girl of feeling had to rush up stairs in a torrent of grief. Yearning after sympathy and love, neither felt nor understood by the minds with whom she herded, a trio of worldliness, apathy, and coarse brutality, her bosom ached as an empty void: treated with habitual neglect and cold indifference, made various (as occasion might present) by stern rebuke or bitter sarcasm, her heart was sore within its cell, and the poor dear child lived a life of daily martyrdom, her feelings smitten upon the desecrated altar of home by the "foes of her own household."

And not least hostile in the band of those home-foes was this only brother, John. Look at him as he stands alone there, muttering after her as she ran up stairs, "Plague take the girl!" and let me tell you what I know of him.

That thick-set form, with its pock-marked face, imprisons as base a spirit as Baal's. He was a chip of the old block, and something more. If the father had a heart with "gold" written on it, the son had no heart at all, but gold was in its place. Thoroughly unscrupulous as to ways and means, and simply acting on the phrase "*quocunque modo rem*," he seemed to have neither conscience of evil, nor dread of danger. In two words, he was a "bold bad" man, divested equally of fear and feeling. The memoirs of his past life hitherto, without controversy very little edifying, may be guessed with quite sufficient accuracy for all characteristic purposes from the coarse, sensual, worldly, and iniquitous result now standing for his portraiture before us. We will waste on such a type of heartlessness as few words as possible: let his conduct show the man.

Just now, this worthy had risen into high favour with his father: we already know why; he had suddenly got rich on his own account, and for that very sufficient reason drew any additional sums he pleased on "the governor's." The trick or two, whereat Sir Thomas hinted, and which so wise a man would not have blabbed to fools, are worthy of record; not merely as illustrative of character, but (in one case at least, as we may find hereafter) for the sake of ulterior consequences.

John Dillaway's first exploit in the money-making line was a clever one. He managed to possess himself of a carrier-pigeon of the Antwerp breed, one among a flock kept for stock-jobbing purposes, by a certain great capitalist; and he contrived that this trained bird should wheel down among the merchants just at noon one fine day in the Royal Exchange. The billet under its wing contained certain cabalistic characters, and the plain-spoken intelligence, "*Louis Philippe est mort!*" In a minute after these most revolutionizing news, French funds, then at one hundred and twelve, were toppling down below ninety, and our prudent John was buying stock in all directions: nay, he even made some considerable bargains at eighty-seven. There was a complete panic in the market, and wretched was the man who possessed French fives. The afternoon's work so beautifully finished, John spent that night as true-born Britons are reported to have done before the battle of Hastings, rioting in drunken bliss, and panting for the morrow; and when the morrow came, and the Paris post with it, I must leave it to be understood with what complacency of triumph our enterprising stock-jobber hastened to sell again at one hundred and fourteen, pocketing, in the aggregate, a difference of several thousand pounds. It was a feat altogether to ravish a delighted father's heart, and no wonder that he counted John so great a comfort.

Martin Farquhar Tupper

Trick number two had been at once even more lucrative and more dangerous. As a stock-broker, this enterprising Mr. Dillaway had peculiar opportunities of investigating closely certain records in the office for unclaimed dividends: he had an object in such close inspection, and discovered soon that one Mrs. Jane Mackenzie, of Ballyriggan, near Belfast, was a considerable proprietor, and had made no claim for years. Why should so much money lie idle? Was the woman dead? Probably not; for in that case executors or administrators would have touched it. Legatees and next of kin are little apt to forget such matters. Well, then, if this Mrs. Jane Mackenzie is alive, she must be a careless old fool, and we'll try if we can't kill her on paper, and so come in for spoils instead of kith and kin. "Shrewd Jack," as they called him in the Alley, chuckled within himself at so feasible a plot.

Accordingly, in an artful and well-concocted way, which we may readily conceive, but it were weary to detail, John Dillaway managed to forge a will of Jane Mackenzie aforesaid; and inducing some dressed-up "ladies" of his acquaintance to personate the weeping nieces of deceased (doubtless with no lack of Irish witnesses beside, competent to swear to any thing), he contrived to pass probate at Doctors' Commons, and get twelve thousand two hundred and forty-three pounds, bank annuities transferred, as per will, to the two ladies legatees. As the munificent *douceur* of a thousand pounds a-piece had (for the present) stopped the mouths of those supposititious nieces, who stipulated for not a farthing more nor less, clever John Dillaway a second time had the filial opportunity of rejoicing his father's heart by this wholesale money-making. Ten thousand pounds bank stock was manifestly another good day's work; and seeing our John had not appeared at all in the transaction, even as the ladies' stock-broker, things were made so safe, that the chuckling knight, when he heard all this (albeit he did tenderly fy, fy a little at first), was soon induced to think "my son Jack" the very best boy and the very cleverest dog in Christendom: at once a parent's pride and joy. Yes, Lady Dillaway—such a comfort! And the worshipful stationer apostrophized "rich Jack" with lips that seemed to smack of Creasy's Brighton sauce, whilst his calm spouse appeared to acquiesce in her amiable John's good fortune. The mystified mother little guessed that it was felony.

This good son's new-born wealth, besides the now liberal paternal largess (for his allowance grew larger in proportion as he might seem to need it less), of course availed to introduce him to some fashionable and estimable circles of society, whither it might not at all times be discreet in us to follow him; amongst other places, whether or not the Pandemonium in Jermyn street proved to him another gold mine, we have not yet heard; but John Dillaway was often there, the intimate friend of many splendid cavaliers who lived upon their industry, familiar with a whole rookery of blacklegs, patron of two or three pigeonable city sparks, and, on the whole, flusher of money than ever. His quiet mother, if she cared about her son at all, and probably she did care when her health permitted, might well be apprehensive on the score of that increasing wealth which made the father's joy.

However, with all his prosperity Mr. John as yet professed himself by no means satisfied; he was far too greedy of gain, and ever since he had come to man's estate, had amiably longed to be an only child. Not that he heeded a monopoly of the parental feelings and affections, nor even that he meditated murdering Maria—oh dear, no: rather too troublesome that, and quite unnecessary; it would be entirely sufficient if he could manage so to influence his father as to cut that superfluous sister Maria very short indeed in the matter of cash. With this generous and amiable view, he now for a course of sundry years had whispered, back-bitten, and lied; he had, as occasion offered, taken mean advantages of Maria's outspeaking honesty, had set her warm-hearted sayings and charitable doings in the falsest lights, and had entirely "mildewed the ear" of her listening papa. The knight in truth listened unreluctantly; it was consolation, if not happiness to him, if he could make or find excuses for harshness to a being who would not worship wealth; it would be joy and pride, and an honour to his idol, if he should keep Maria pretty short of cash, and so make her own its preciousness; triumphant would he feel, as a merely-moneyed man, to see troublesome, obtrusive Heart, with all its win-ways, and whimperings, and incomprehensible spirituality, with its sermons and its prayers, bending before him "for a bit of bread." Yes, poor loving disinterested Maria ran every chance of being disinherited, from the false witness of her brother, simply because she gave him antecedent opportunities, by her honest likings and dislikings, by her bold rebuke of wrong and open zeal for right, by her scorn of hypocrisies as to what she did feel, or did not feel, and by the unpopular fact that she wore a heart, and refused to be the galley-slave of gold.

"Oh, ho, then!" said our crafty John, "we shall soon set this all right with our governor; thank you for the chance, Miss Maria. If father doesn't kick out this Clements, and cut you off with a shilling, he is not Sir Thomas, and I am not his son."

CHAPTER VII

PROVIDENCE SEES FIT TO HELP VILLANY

"Now that's what I call bones."

It was a currish image, suggestive of the choicest satisfaction. Let us try to discover what good news such an
idiosyncrasy as that of John Dillaway would be pleased to
designate as "bones." He had forthwith gone to his father's
room as merry at the chance of ousting poor Maria, as the
heartlessness of avarice could make him; and omnipresent
authorship jotted down the dialogue that follows:

"So, governor, there's to be a wedding here, I find; when
does it come off?"

"Ey? what? a wedding? whose?"

"Oh, ho! you don't know, ey? I guessed as much: what do
you think now of our laughing, and crying, and kissing, and
praying Miss Maria with—

"Not that beggar Clements? Ey? what? d—" &c., &c.

"Ha, ha, ha, ha! I thought so; why not, governor? Are you an
old mole, that you haven't seen it these six weeks? Are you

Martin Farquhar Tupper

stone deaf, that all their pretty speeches have been wasted on you? All I can say is, that if Mr. and Mrs. Clements an't spliced, it's pretty well time they should be, and—

"Sir Thomas Dillaway rattled out so terrible an oath about Maria's disinheritance if she ventured upon a marriage, that even John was staggered at such a dreadful curse; nevertheless, an instantaneous reflection soon caused that curse to be viewed metaphorically as a 'bone;' and the generous brother cautiously proceeded—

"Why, governor, all this is very odd, must say; when I caught 'em kissing up there ten minutes ago, they were sharp enough to swear that you knew all about it, and that you were so 'very, very kind.'"

How is it possible, intelligent reader, to avoid perpetual allusion to an oath? We must not pare the lion's claws, and give bad men soft speeches: pr'ythee, supply an occasional interjection, and believe that in this place Sir Thomas swore most awfully; then, in a complete phrensy, he vowed that he "would turn Maria out of house and home this minute." This was another "bone," clearly.

But it was now becoming politic to calm him. Shrewd Jack was well aware that Maria would relinquish all, and sacrifice, not merely her own heart, but her Henry's too, rather than be guilty of filial disobedience. All this storming, hopeful as it looked, might still be premature, and do no substantial good; nay, if this wrath broke out too soon, Maria would at once give way, become more dutiful than ever, and his golden chance was gone. No: they were not married yet. Let the wedding somehow first take place, and then—! and then!—for now he knew which way the wind blew; so the scheming youth calmed his rising triumphs, and counselled his progenitor as follows:

"Well, governor, I never saw so green a blade in all my born days. Can't you see, now, that it's all cram this, just to put you in spirits, old boy, in case of such things happening? It was wicked too of me to tease you so—but I'm so jolly, governor; such luck in Jermyn street—I knew you'd like a joke served up with such rich sauce as this is, ey? only look!" It was half a hatful of bank notes raked up at the hazard table.

Sir Thomas's gray eyes darted swiftly at the spoil; often as he had warned and scolded Jack about the matter of Jermyn street (for Jack was bold enough never to conceal one of his little foibles), the father had now nothing to object; for, in his philosophy, the end justified the means. With most of this wise world, he looked upon success as in the nature of virtue, and failure as the surest sign of vice; accordingly his ire was diverted on the moment, and blazed in admiration of son Jack: and that estimable creature immediately determined it was wise to speak in tones of unwonted affection respecting his sister.

"Now, governor, I put it to you plump, isn't this hatful enough to make a man beside himself, so as not to stick at a white lie or two? Dear Maria there is no more going to become a Mrs. Clements than you are; she cut the fellow dead long ago: so mind, that's a tough old bird, you don't say one word to her about him; it would be just raking up the cinders again, you know, and you might be fool enough to raise a flame. No, governor, if it's any consolation to you, that pauper connection has been all at an end this month; not but what the beggar's got my mother's ear still, I fancy; but as to Maria, she detests him. So take my advice, and don't tease the poor girl about the business. Now, then, that this is all settled, and now that you 're the merrier for that silly bit of storming at nothing, just listen: the wedding's my own! isn't Jack Dillaway a clever fellow now, to have caught a

Right Honourable Ladyship, with a park in Yorkshire, a palace in Wales, and a mansion in Grosvenor square?"

At this *extempore* invention, the delighted parent rained so many blessings on his progeny, that John knew the tide was turned at once. Our ex-lord mayor had high ambitions, dating from the year of glory onwards; so that nothing could be more prudent or well-timed that this ideal aristocratic connection. Jack was a good fellow, a dear boy; and he added to his apparent amiabilities now by reiterating counsels of kindness and silence towards "poor dear sister Maria, whom he had been making the scape-goat all this time;" after which done, our stock-jobber feigned a pressing engagement with some fashionable friends, and left his father to ruminate upon his worth in lonely admiration.

Well; if that clever and gratuitous lie was not another "bone," I am at a loss to know what could be a "bone" to such a hound: therefore it appears that Dillaway had three of them at least to gladden him in solitude; and he went on revealing to wonder-stricken angels, and to us, the secrets of his crafty soul, as he thus soliloquized:

"Yes, marry the fools first, and then for spoils at leisure; it won't be easy though, she's so consummate filial, and he so bloated up with honour. They'll never wed, I'm clear, unless the governor's by to bless 'em; and as to managing that, and the cutting-adrift scheme too, one kills the other. How the deuce to do it? Eh—do I see a light?"

He did. A light lurid sulphurous gleam upon the midnight of his mind seemed to show the way before him, as wisp-fire in a marsh. He did see a light, and its character was this:

Quite aware of his mother's tranquil hopefulness, and that his kind good sister was ingenuous as the day, he soon apprehended the state of affairs; and, resolving to increase those misunderstandings on all sides, he quickly perceived that he could triumph in the keen Machiavellian policy, "*divide et impera*." The plan became more obvious as he calmly thought it out. Evidently his first step must be to ingratiate himself with both Henry and Maria, as the sympathizing brother, a very easy task among such charitable fools: number two should be to persuade them, as the mother did, that Sir Thomas, generally a reserved unsocial man at home (and that in especial to Maria), was very nervous at the thought of losing his dear daughter, and (while he acquiesced in the common fate of parents and the usual way of the world) begged that his coming bereavement might be obtruded on him as little as possible—Mr. Clements always to avoid him, and Maria to hold her tongue: number three, to amuse his father all the while by the prospect of his own high alliance, so as effectually to hoodwink him from what was going on: and, number four, to send him up to Yorkshire a week hence (on some fool's errand to inquire after the imaginary countess's imaginary mortgages), leaving behind him an autograph epistle (which our John well knew how to write), recommending "that the ceremony be performed immediately and in his absence, to spare his feelings on the spot," mentioning "son John as his worthy substitute to give dear Maria away," and enclosing them at once his "blessing and a hundred pound note to help them on their honeymoon."

"John Dillaway, if craft be a virtue, thou art an archangel: but if Heaven's chief requirement is the heart, thou art very like a devil—very. If selfishness deserves the meed of praise, who more honourable than thou art? But if a heartless man can never reach to happiness, I know who will live to curse the hour of his birth, and is doomed to perish miserably."

It was a clever scheme, and had unscrupulous hands to work

it. Mystified by quiet Lady Dillaway as our lovers had been from the first, entirely unsuspicious of all guile, and rejoicing in their brother's marvellous amiability, never surely were such happy days; always together while the knight was at his counting-house, they gladly acquiesced in his beautifully paternal nervousness; it was a delightful trait of character in the dear old man; and a very respectable proof that love is keen-eyed enough to believe what it wishes, but is stone-blind to any thing that might possibly counteract its hopes. Then again, the mother was a close ally; for having set her quiet heart upon the match, Lady Dillaway at once encouraged all John's sympathetic scheme, on the prudent principle of getting the young couple inextricably married first, and then obliging her lord to be reconciled afterwards to what he could not help. Sir Thomas himself, poor blinkered creature, was full of the most aristocratical and wealthy fancies, and only yearned to inspect the acres of his future honourable grand-children. He was, from these fanciful causes, unusually affable and indulgent to Maria; spoke so kindly always that she was all but dissolving thrice a-day; and, from his constant reveries about the countess, appeared perpetually to be brooding over dear Maria's soon approaching loss. Poor girl! more than once she had determined to give it all up, and make her father happy by serving him still in single blessedness: but then, how could she break dear Henry's heart, as well as her own? No, no: they should live very near to Finsbury square, and be in and out constantly, and papa should never miss her: how delightful was all this!

As for John himself, (our heartless model-man, strange contrast to Maria's perfect charity!) he chuckled hugely as his scheme now ripened fast. He had long been putting all things in train for the wedding to-morrow. Every body knew it except Sir Thomas who—what between Jack's prudent watchfulness, his habitual counting-house hours, his usually unsocial silence, and his now asserted wish for "not one word upon the subject,"—was at once kept in total ignorance of all; and yet, as ambassadorial John constantly gave out to Clements and Maria, in an amiable nervous state of natural acquiescence. Next day, then, the besotted father was about to be packed post for Yorkshire; the important letter, with its enclosed bank note, was already written and sealed, as like the governor's hand as possible; a license had been long ago provided, and the clergyman bespoke, by the brotherly officiousness of John; neither Henry Clements, who was too delicate, too unsuspecting for prudent business-papers, nor Maria, whose heart was never likely to have conceived the thought, had even once alluded to a settlement; Lady Dillaway was lying, as her wont was, on her habitual sofa, in tranquil ecstasy, at to-morrow morning's wedding: and Holy Providence, for wise purposes no doubt, had seen fit to aid a villain in his deep-laid treacherous designs.

The Wednesday dawned: Sir Thomas was to be off early, poor man, all agog for right honourable acres; and Maria could no longer restrain the expression of her glad and grateful feelings. Up she got by six, threw herself in her kind dear father's way; and though, to spare his feelings, she said not a word about the marriage, prayed him on her knees for a blessing. The startled parent, believing all this frantic show of feeling was sufficiently to be accounted for by his own long and no doubt dangerous journey, blessed her as devoutly as ever he could; and when the carriage drove away, left her in his study, overcome with joy, affection, and admiration of his fine heart, exquisite sensibilities, and generous feelings. Then, as a crowning-stone to all the bliss, if any lingering doubt existed in the mind of Clements, who had more than once expressed dislike at Sir Thomas's silent and unsatisfying sympathy—the letter—the letter, whereof kind brother John, secretly initiated, had some days forewarned them of its probability—that letter, which explained at once all a father's kind anxieties, and made up for all his cold reserve, was found on Sir Thomas's own table! How amiable, how beautifully sensitive, how liberal too! Lady Dillaway plumed herself in a whispering transport upon her just appreciation of the father's better feelings; a kinder heart manifestly never existed than her husband's, though he did take strange methods of proving it: the bridesmaids, two daughters of a friend and neighbour, privy to the coming mystery three days, approved highly of so unobtrusive an old gentleman: Maria was all pantings, blushings, weepings, and rejoicings; Henry Clements, handsome, pale, and agitated; perhaps, misgiving too, and a little displeased at the father's absence; however, Mr. John Dillaway gave away the bride with a most paternal air; and, just as Sir Thomas was changing horses at Huntingdon, our innocent lovers were indissolubly married.

CHAPTER VIII

THE ROGUE'S TRIUMPH

Never was there such a happy couple; nor a more auspicious day. Away they went, in deep delight, too joyful to be merry, in a holy transport of affection, and its dearest hope fulfilled. They seemed to be in love with all the world, for every thing around them wore a lustre of deliciousness: and when the smoking posters left them at Salt hill, and that well-matched husband and wife sat down to their first boiled fowl, it would probably be a bathos to allude to angelic bliss; but they nevertheless were, and knew they were, the happiest of mortals. If any thing could add to Henry's self-complacency at that moment, it was the recollection of his own truly disinterested conduct; for only yesterday he had transferred all his little property to that kind and brotherly fellow John Dillaway, in trust for Maria Clements, should any possible reverse of fortune affect her father's or his own prosperity. Yes; and John had been so wise as to make the two hundred a-year already a third more, by investing (as he said) what had been a few thousands of three per cents. in some capital "independent" bank shares of Australasia—safe as a mountain, and productive as a valley.

All this appeared very prosperous and pleasant: but we of the initiated into the secrets of character, may reasonably

　　　　　Martin Farquhar Tupper

apprehend that Henry's little all would have been safer any where than in Dillaway's possession: and "possession," I am sorry to declare, is a word used advisedly; for Mr. John required a largish floating capital to enable him to go to the desperate lengths he did at hazard and *rouge-et-noir*; and I am afraid that if Mr. or Mrs. Clements were to receive any of those so-called Austral dividends, they would only have been taking three hundred pounds a-year out of their principal moneys in John's immaculate keeping.

Leaving then those wedded lovers to their honey-moon of joy, and shrewd Jack gloating not merely over the full success of his nefarious plan, but also over this unexpected acquisition of poor Clement's few thousands, let us return to Sir Thomas—or, to be quite accurate, let us return with him.

In high dudgeon, full of fire and fury, back rushed the knight, sore under the sense of having been made an April-fool of in July; for no one in the place whereto he went, had ever heard of a widow'd Countess of Lancing; and her ladyship's acres, if any where at all, were undoubtedly not in the North Riding. But clever son John, meeting his indignant father on the threshold, soon made all that right by a word.

"Well, if ever! why, stupid, I said Diddlington, not Darlington."

Into the accuracy of this distinction it is needless to inquire: and then the ingenuous youth went on to observe—

"But all's right as it is now; you may as well not have seen the property, and better, too, as things have turned out roughly, governor: the match is off, and you may well congratulate me. Such an escape—I just discovered it, and was barely in time: you hadn't been gone two hours when I found it all out, through a clever devil of a lawyer, who was hired by my father's son to look into incumbrances, and keep a sharp look-out for a mutual settlement; that old harridan of a ladyship is over head and ears in debt; and, it seems, I was to have paid all straight, or *i. e.* you, governor, ey? As to the Yorkshire acres, the old woman had but a life interest in the mere bit that wasn't deeply mortgaged—and not a very long life either, seeing she is seventy. So, bless your clever boy again, old governor, he's free."

The knight had nothing to object: Jack's ready lie had plenty of reasons in it: and so he blessed his clever boy again.

"But I say, governor, I rather think that you've astonished us all: what on earth made you turn so soft of a sudden, and write that letter?"

"What letter? ey? what?"—Sir Thomas might well inquire.

"That's a good joke, governor—you keep it up to the last, I see; what a close old file it is! What letter? why, the letter you wrote to Maria and her lord, telling them to marry."

"Marry? ey? what, Maria? what—what is it all?" The poor old man was thoroughly bewildered.

"Well done, governor—bravo! you can carry it off as cleverly as if you were an actor; do you mean to say now you didn't leave a letter behind you here upon your table, bidding Maria marry in your absence to spare your paternal feelings (kind old boy, it is, too!) and enclosing them one hundred pounds for the honey-moon?"

The mystified father made some inarticulate expression of ignorant amazement, and our stock-jobber went on:

"So of course they're married and off—Mr. and Mrs. Cle—"

A whirlwind of disastrous imprecations cut all short; and then in a voice choked with passion he gasped out—

"But—but are they married—are they married? how do you know it? can't we catch 'em first, ey? what!"

"How do I know it? that's a good un now, father, when I had it under your hand to give the girl away myself instead of you. Do you mean to say you didn't write that letter?"

"Boy, I tell you, I've written nothing—I know nothing; you speak in riddles."

"Well then, governor, if I do, I'll to guess 'em: I begin to see how it was all brought about—but they did it cleverly too, and were quite too many for me. Only listen: that fellow Clements, ay, and Miss Maria too (artful minx, I know her), must have forged a letter as if from you to get poor fools, me and my mother, to see 'em spliced, while you were tooling to Yorkshire."

"Impossible—ey? what? I'll—I'll—I'll—"

"Now, governor, don't stand there doing nothing but denying all I say; only you go yourself, and ask my mother if she didn't see the letter—if they didn't marry upon it, and if that precious sister of mine doesn't richly deserve every thing she'll some day get from her affectionate, her excellent, her ill-used father?"

Iago's self, or his master, smooth-tongued Belial, could not have managed matters better.

The incredulous knight, scarcely able to discover how far it might not still be all a joke, especially after his Yorkshire expedition, rushed up to Lady Dillaway; on her usual sofa, quietly knitting, and thinking of her Maria's second day of happiness.

"So, ma'am—ey? what? is it true? are they married? is it true? married—ey? what?"

"Certainly, Thomas, they were only too glad, and I will add, so was I, to get your kind—"

"Mine? I give leave? ey? what? Madam, we're cheated, fooled—I never wrote any letter."

"Most astonishing; I saw it myself, Thomas, your own hand; and our dear John too."

"Ay, ay—he sees through it all, and so do I now—ey? what? that precious pair of rogues forged it! Now, ma'am, what don't they deserve, I should like to know?"

It was quite a blow, and a very hard one, to the poor tranquil mother. Could her dear Maria really have been so base, and that noble-looking Henry too? how dreadfully deceived in them, if this proved true! And how could she think it false? A letter contrived to expedite their marriage in the father's casual absence, which no one could have thought of writing but Sir Thomas himself, or the impatient lovers. So poor Lady Dillaway could only fall a-crying very miserably; whereupon her husband more than half suspected her of being an accomplice in the despicable plot.

"Now then, ma'am, I'm determined: as they are married, the thing's at an end; we can't untie that knot—but, once tied, I've done with the girl; they may starve, for any help they'll get of me: and as for you, mum, give 'em money at your peril; stay, to make sure of it, Lady Dillaway, I shall stint you to whatever you choose to ask me for out of my own pocket; never draw another cheque on Jones's, do you hear? ey? what? for your cheques shall not be honoured, ma'am. And now, from this hour, you and I have only one child, John."

"Oh, Thomas—Thomas! be merciful to poor Maria! indeed, she was deceived; she believed it all—poor Maria!"

"Ma'am, never mention that woman again—ey? what? deceived? Yes, she deceived you and me, and John, and all. Wicked wretch! and all to marry a beggar! Well, ma'am, there's one comfort left; the fellow married her for money, and he's caught in his own trap; never a penny of mine shall either of them see. Henceforth, Lady Dillaway, we have no daughter; dear John is the only child left us for old age."

In spite of himself, of wrath, and disappointment, the father spoke in a moved and broken manner; and his weeping wife attempted to explain, console, and soothe him; but all in vain—he was inexorable and inveterate against those mean deceivers. To say truth, the poor mother was staggered too, especially when her managing son set all the matter in what he stated to be the right light; for he had, the whole business through, whispered so separately to each, and had seemed to say so little openly (making his mother believe that his sister told him of the coming letter, and a choice variety of other embellishments), that he was now looked upon as the very martyr to roguish plotting, in having been induced to give away his sister. Excellent, mistaken John!

And forthwith John became installed sole heir, proving the most dutiful of sons: how glibly would he tell them any sort of welcome news, original or selected; how many anecdotes could he invent to prove his own merits and certain other folks' deficiencies; how amiably would he fetch and carry slippers and smelling-bottles, and write notes, and read newspapers, and make himself every thing by turns (he devoutly hoped it would be nothing long) to his poor dear parents, as became an only child! It was quite affecting—and both father and mother, softened in spite of themselves at the loss of that Maria, often would talk over the new-found virtues of their most exemplary son. His character came out now with five-fold lustre when contrasted with his former usual ruggedness: no widow ever had a one sick child more tender, more considerate, more dutiful, than rude Jack Dillaway.

He gained his end; saw the new will signed; earwigged the lawyer; and kept a copy of it.

CHAPTER IX

FALSE-WITNESS KILLS A MOTHER,
AND WOULD WILLINGLY STARVE A SISTER

Day by day, letters, doubtless full of happiness and Heart, were left by the promiscuous and undiscerning postman at the house in Finsbury square, from our excellent calumniated couple; but, seeing that there were always two sieves waiting ready to sift it before it came to Lady Dillaway's turn—to wit, John in the hall, and Sir Thomas in his study, it came to pass that every letter with those malefactors' hand and seal on it got burnt instanter, and unopened.

How many troubles might mankind be spared if they would only stop to hear each other's explanations! How many ailments, both of body and soul, if explanations only came more frequently and freely! Melancholy from that dreadful doubt, and all these cold delays, viewing her daughter as a criminal, the husband as a swindler, and all this long course of silence as very, very heartless and seemingly conclusive of their guilt, the poor mother sickened fast upon her couch: she had for years always been an invalid, wan and wo-begone, living upon ether, gum, and chicken-broth; but her white skin now grew whiter, her faint voice fainter, the energies of life in her debilitated frame weaker than ever; it was no mere hypochondria, or other fanciful malady: her calm heart seemed to be dying down within her, as a plant that has earth-grubs gnawing at its root—she grew very ill. Days, weeks of silence—her heart was sick with hope deferred. How could Maria, with all her seeming warmth, treat her with such utter negligence? But now the honey-moon was coming to an end: they must call and see her some day again, surely; how strangely unkind not to answer those motherly and anxious letters, sent to their first known stage, Salt hill, and thereafter to be forwarded.

O, cold continued crime! Bad man, bad man, thy mother's own hand-writing shall plead against thee at the last dread day. For those coveted letters of affection, often sent on both those loving parts, had been regularly and ruthlessly intercepted, opened, mocked, and burnt! How could the man have stood case-proof against those letters—his mother's anxious outbursts of affection towards a lost, an innocent, a calumniated sister? For selfishness had dried up in that hard and wily man all the milk of human kindness.

And our loving pair, upon their travels, were as much hurt and surprised at this long silence as poor Lady Dillaway herself: it was most mysterious, inexplicable. The only letter they had received ever since they had left home was one—only one, from John, which had frightened them exceed-ingly. Some practical joker (the bridesmaid's brother was suspected), by way of giving Maria a present on her approa-ching wedding, as it would seem, had cleverly imitated her father's hand-writing, and—that letter was a forgery! to every body's great amazement. Nobody could, according to his own account, be kinder than John, who had done more than mortal things to appease his father; but the old man remained implacable. It was a meanly-contrived clandestine match, he said; and he never intended to set eyes on them again! As for John, he in that letter had strongly counselled them to keep away, and trust to him for bringing his father round. In the midst of their terrible dilemma, kind brother John seemed as an angel sent by Heaven to assist them.

Dear children of affection and calamity! how innocently did they walk into the snare; and how closely doth the wicked man draw his toils around them. Who can accuse them of any wrong (the hopefulness of love considered) in point either of honour or duty? And shall they not be righted at the last? It may be so—it shall be so: but Holy Providence hath purposes of good in plunging those twin wedded hearts deep beneath the billows of earthly destitution. The wicked must prosper for a while, in this as in a million other cases, and the good for their season struggle with adversity; that the one may be destroyed for ever, and the others may add to this world's wealth the incalculable riches of another.

They had spent the few first weeks of marriage among the pleasant lakes and hills of Westmoreland and Cumberland, wandering together, in delightful interchange of thought, from glen to glen, from tairn to tairn, all about Ambleside, Helvellyn, and Lodore, Ullswater, Saddleback, and Schiddaw. Maria's ever-flickering smile seemed to throw a sun-beam over the darkest moor, even in those darkest hours of doubt, heart-sickening anxiety, and grief at the neglect which they experienced; while Henry's well-informed good sense not only availed to cheer the sad Maria, but made every rock a point of interest, and showed every little flower a miracle of wisdom. There were hundreds of extemporaneous "lover's seats," where they had "rested, to be thankful" for the past, joyful for the present, and hopeful for the future; and every ramble that they took might deservedly take the name, style, and title of a "lover's walk!" Happy times—happy times! but still there might be happier; yes, and happiest, too, they seemed to whisper, if ever they should have a merry little nursery of prattling boys and girls! But I am not so entirely in the confidence of those young folks as to be certain about what they seemed to whisper: in that pretty prattling sentence were they not getting a little beyond the honey-moon? Yes—yes, young Hymen is too full of new-found pleasure to heed those holier joys of calm old marriage; for wedded love is as a coil of line, lengthening with the lapse of years, fitted and intended, day after day, to be continually sounding a lower and a lower deep in the ocean of happiness.

Returned to town, it was the immediate care of our fond, confused, and unfortunate young couple to call at the old house in Finsbury square; where, to their great dismay and misery, they encountered a formal standing order for their non-admission. The domestics were new, had been strictly warned against the name of Clements, and, in effect, were creatures of the worthy John. It was a deplorable business; they did not know what to think, nor how to act. Letters left at the door, couched in whatever terms of humility, kindliness, and just excuse, were equally unavailing; for the Cerberus there was too well sopped by pleasant brother John ever to deliver them to any one but him. It was entirely hopeless—extraordinary—a most wretched state of things. What were they to do? The only practicable mode of getting at Sir Thomas, and, therefore, at some explanation of these mysteries, was obviously to watch for him, and meet him in the street. As for Lady Dillaway, she was very ill, and kept her chamber, which was as resolutely guarded from incursion or excursion as Danae's herself—yea, more so, for gold was added to her guards: Sir Thomas, going to and from his counting-house, appeared to be the only weak point in the enemy's fortifications.

Poor old man! he was, or thought he was, harder, colder, more inveterate than ever: and his duteous son John rarely let him venture out alone, for fear of some such meeting, casual or intended. Accordingly, one day when the Clements and

Martin Farquhar Tupper

the Dillaways mutually spied each other afar off, and a junction seemed inevitable, John's promptitude bade his father (generously as it looked, for paternal peace of mind's sake) return a few paces, get into a cab, and so slip home, the while he valiantly stepped forward to meet the enemy.

"Mr. Clements! my father (I grieve to say) will hear no reason, nor any excuse whatever; he totally refuses to see you or Mrs. Clements."

"O, dearest John! what have I done—what has Henry done, that papa, and you, and dear mamma, should all be so unkind to us?"

"You have married, Mrs. Clements, contrary to your father's wish and knowledge: and he has cast you off—I must say—deservedly."

"Brother, brother! you know I was deceived, and Henry too. This is cruel, most cruel: let me see my beloved father but one moment!"

"His commands are to the contrary, madam; and I at least obey them. Henceforth you are a stranger to us all."

The poor broken-hearted girl fell into her husband's arms, stone-white: but her hard brother, making no account whatever of all that show of feeling, only took the trouble quietly to address Henry Clements. "Misfortunes never come single, they say; it is no fault of mine if the proverb hits Mr. Henry Clements. I am sorry to have to tell you, sir, that the Austral Independent bank has stopped payment, and is not expected to refund to its depositors or shareholders one penny in the pound."

"Impossible, Mr. Dillaway! You answered for its stability

yourself: and the proposition came originally from you. I hope surely, surely, you may have been misinformed of these bad news."

"It is true, sir—too true for you: the wisest man on 'change is often out of reckoning. I have nothing now of yours in my hands, sir: you are aware that no writings passed between us."

"Great Heaven! be just and merciful! Are we, then, to be utterly ruined?"

"Really, sir, you know your own affairs better than I can.— Your servant, Mr. Clements."

O, hard and wicked heart!—what will not such a miscreant do for money? Nothing, I am clear, but the cowardly fear of discovery prevents John Dillaway from becoming a positive parricide by very arsenic or razor, so as to grasp his cheated father's will and wealth. And this assertion will appear not in the least uncharitable, when the reader is in this place reminded that Henry Clements's own little property had never been Australized at all, but was still safe and snug in the coffers of crafty John. Jermyn street—or the sharpers congregated there—had drained him very considerably; all his own ill-got gains had been gradually raked away by the croupier at the gaming-table; and unsuspecting Henry's little trust-fund was to be the next bank on which the brother played.

Poor Henry and Maria! What will they do? where will they go? how will they live? Hard questions all, not to be answered in a hurry. We shall see. There was one comfort, though, amidst all their misery;—they did not find the adage a true one, which alludes to poverty coming in at the door, and love flying out of the window; for they never loved each other more deeply—more devotedly—than when daily bread was growing a scarcity, and daily life almost a burden. But we are anticipating.

And how fared the parents all this while? was the erring daughter entirely forgotten? No, no. Son John, indeed, took good care to hinder any amicable feelings of relapse to intrude upon his father's resolution. But the old man was not easy, nevertheless; often thought of poor Maria; and could not clearly make out who had forged the letter. Had it not been for that wicked brother John, a meeting—an explanation—a reconciliation—would undoubtedly have taken place: but he was shrewd enough to keep them asunder, and did not take much to heart his father's altered spirits and breaking state of health: his will and wealth were seemingly all the nearer.

And what of that poor stricken mother? Wasted to a shadow, feverish and weak, she lay for weeks, counting the dreary hours, till she heard of dear, though unnatural, Maria. Oh! the heartless caitiff, John! will he thus watch his mother die by inches, when one true word from his lips could restore her to tranquillity and health? Yes, he would—he did—the wretch! She gradually pined—waned—wasted; the candle of her life burnt down into the hollow socket—glimmering awhile—flared and reeled, and then—one night, quietly and suddenly—went out! She entered on the world of spirits, where all secrets show revealed; and there she read, almost before she died—whilst yet the black curtain of eternity was gradually rising to receive her—the innocence of good Maria, and the deep-stained villany of John. Her last words—uttered supernaturally from her quiescence, with the fervour of a visionary whose ken is more than mortal—were "Look, look, Thomas!—beware of John. O poor, poor innocent outcast!—O rich, rich heart of love—Maria! my Mari—a—!"

CHAPTER X

HOW TO HELP ONE'S SELF

Where then did they live, and how—that noble and calumniated couple? They had done no wrong, nor even, as it seems to us, the semblance of wrong, unless it be by having acquiesced in the foolishness of secresy, and thus aided the contrivance of false witness; for aught else, their only social error had been lack of business caution among business men. Feeling generously themselves, they gave others credit for the like good feeling; acting upon honourable impulse, they believed that other men would act so too. Heart was the hindrance in their way;—too much sensitiveness towards all about them; too swift a surrender of the judgment to the affections: too imprudent a reliance upon other men of the world; though, when they trusted to a father's love, and a brother's honesty, prudence herself might have almost been dispensed with. Machinations of the wicked and the shrewd hemmed them in to their un-doing: and really, they, children more or less of affluent homes, born and bred in plenty, who had moved all their lives long in circles of comparative wealth and wastefulness, now seemed likely to come to the galling want of necessary sustenance. Was it not to teach them deeper feeling for the poor, if ever God again should give them riches? Was it not, by poverty, to try those hearts which had passed so blamelessly through all the ordeals and temptations of wealth, in order that they worthily might wear the double crown given only to such as remain unhardened by prosperity, unembittered by adversity? Was it not to discipline our warm Maria's love, and to chasten her Henry's very gentlemanly pride into the due Christian proportions— self-respect with self-humiliation? Was it not, chiefest and best, to school their hearts for heaven, and, by feeding them on miseries and wrongs a little while, to fix their affections on things above rather than on things of this world? Yes: Providence has many ends in view, and they all tend consistently to one great focus—the ultimate advantage of the good by means of the confusion of the wicked.

Meanwhile came trouble on apace. Henry Clements justly felt aggrieved, insulted; and the sentiment of pride, improper only from excess, determined him to make no more advances: all that man could do, that is, which a gentleman ought to do, he had done; but letters and visits proved equally unavailing. He had come to the resolution that he would make no more efforts himself, nor scarcely let Maria make any. As for her, poor soul! she was now in grievous tribulation, with sad, sufficient reason for it too; seeing that, in addition to her father's anger, still protracted—in addition to that vile forgery imputed to her craft, and whereof she had been made the guilty victim—in addition to their own soon pressing money-wants, and that heartless fraud of John's against her husband's little all (though she counted of it only as a luckless speculation)—she had just become acquainted, through the public prints, of her dear good mother's death, even before she had heard of any illness. What bitter pangs were there for her, poor child! That she should have lost that mother just then, without forgiveness, without blessing— whilst all was unexplained, and their whole conduct of affections without guile, wore the hideous mask of base, undutiful contrivance! Cheer up, Maria; cheer up! only in this bad world can innocence be sullied with a doubt: cheer up! the spirit of that mother whom you loved on earth knows it well already; learned it while yet she was leaving the body of her death: cheer up! she is still near you both—dear children of affliction and affection! and God has commissioned her for good to be your ministering angel.

With reference to means of living, they appeared limited at once to a little ready money, and a few personal chattels and trinkets; without so much as one pound of capital to back the young house-keepers, or a shilling's-worth of interest or dividend or earnings coming in for weekly bills. Clements had been utterly confounded in all his economical arrangements by that sudden bitter breach of trust; and, albeit (as we have hinted), his aim in marriage was not money; still, without much of worldly calculation, he might prudently have looked for some provision on Maria's part at least equal to his own: in fact, the fond young couple had reasonably set their hearts upon that golden mean—four hundred a-year to begin with. Now, however, by two fell swoops—brother John's dishonesty and Sir Thomas's resolve of disinheritance—all this rational and moderate expectation had been dashed to atoms; and the cottage of contented competence appeared but as a castle in the clouds—a mere airy matter of undiluted moonshine. Thus, when that happiest of honeymoons had dwindled down the hundred-pound bank-note (shrewd John's well-expended bait) to the fractional part of a ten, and our newly-married pair came to put together their united resources, wherewithal to travel through the world, they could muster but very little:—considering, too, the future, and the promise of an early increase to provide for, forty-seven pounds was not quite a fortune; and a few articles of jewellery did not much increase it.

We need not imagine that Henry calmly acquiesced without a struggle in the roguish fraud which had impoverished him;

but, notwithstanding all his best endeavours, he found, to his dismay, that the case was irremediable: the transfer-books, indeed, were evidence; and equity would give credit for the trust: but that the "Independent bank" had failed was a simple fact; and so long as John stood ready to swear he had invested in it, there was an end to the business. Be sure, shrewd Jack was not likely to leave any thing dubious or unsatisfactory in the affair. Austral papers were easily got at now, cheap as whitey-brown; and for any help the law could give him, poor Henry Clements might as well engage the wind-raising services of a Lapland witch.

He must put his shoulder to the wheel without delay; manifestly, his profession of the law, however unlucrative till now, must be the mighty lever that should raise him quickly to the summit of opulence and fame: and he vigorously set to work, as the briefless are forced to do, inditing a new law-book, which should lift him high in honour with those magnates on the bench; being, as he was, a court-counsel, not a chamber one, an eloquent pleader too (if the world would only give him a hearing), he unluckily took for his thesis the questionable 'Doctrine of Defence;' combating magnanimously on the loftiest moral grounds all manner of received opinions, time-honoured fictions, legitimated quibbles, and other things which (as he was pleased to put it) "render the majesty of the law ridiculous to the ears of common sense, and iniquitous in the sight of Christian judgment." Rash youth! forensic Quixote! better had you plodded on, without this extra industry and skill, in the hopeless idleness and solitude of your Temple garret— better had you burnt your wig and gown outright, with all the airy briefs to come that fluttered round them, than have owned yourself the author of that heretical piece of moral mawkishness—'The Doctrine of Defence, by Henry Clements.'"

He had with difficulty found a publisher—a chilling incident enough in itself, considering an author's feelings for his book-child; and when found, the scarcely satisfactory arrangement was insisted on, of mutual participation in profit and loss: in other parlance, the bookseller pocketing the first, and the author unpocketing the second. Thus it came to pass, that after three months' toil and enormous collation of cases —after extravagant indulgence of the most ardent hopes— glory, good, and gold, consequent instantaneously on this happy publication—after reasonably expecting that judges would quote it in their ermine, and sergeants consult it in their silk—that London would be startled by the event from the humdrum of its ordinary routine—and the wondering world applaud the name of Henry Clements—O, heart-sickening reality! what was the result of his exertions?

"So, that puppy Clements has taken upon himself to put us all to school about whom we may defend, and how, I see— Hang the fellow's impudence!" grunted a fat Old Bailey counsel to his peers, well aware that the luckless author sat nervously within ear-shot.

"I know whose junior that modest swain shall never be;" simpered Sergeant Tiffin.

"The fellow's done for himself," was the simultaneous verdict of a well-wigged band of brothers. And what else they might have added in their charity poor Clements never knew, for he crept away to his garret, stricken with disappointment. There he must encounter other trials of the heart: two or three reviews and newspapers lay upon his table, just sent in by the bookseller, as per order; for they contained, in spirit-stirring print, notices of 'Clements on Defence.' Unluckily for his present peace of mind, poor fellow, the periodicals in question were none of the humaner sort; no kindly encouraging 'Literary Register,' no soft-spoken '*Courtier*,' no patient '*Investigator*,' no generously-indulgent '*Critical Gazette*:' these more amiable journals would be slower in the field—some six weeks hence, perhaps, creeping on with philanthropic sloth: but fiercer prints, which dart hebdomadal wrath at every trembling seeker of their parsimonious praise, had whipt up their malice to deliver the first swift blow against our hapless neophyte in print. Thus, when, with nervous preboding, Henry took up the '*Watchman*,' in eager hope for favour to his poor dear book, he turned quite sick at heart to find the lying verdict run as follows, though the small type in which it spake was a comfort too:

"A careless compilation of insignificant cases, clumsily thrown together, and calculated to set its author high indeed upon the rolls of fame; proving to the world that a Mr. Henry Clements can reason very feebly; that his premises are habitually false; and that presumptuous preaching is the natural accompaniment of extreme ignorance."

By all that worries man, but this was too bad: "careless?"— every word had been a care to him: "clumsy?"—in composition it was Addison's own self: "feeble?"—if he was good for any thing, he was good for logic: "false?"—not one premise but stood on adamant, not one conclusion but it was fixed as fate: "presumptuous?"—it was bold and masculine, certainly, but humble too; here and there almost deferential: "ignorant?"—ye powers that live in looks, testify by thousands how Clements had been studying!—And yet this most lying sentence, a congeries or sorites of untruths, hastily penned by some dyspeptic scribe, who perhaps had barely dipped into the book, was at the moment circulating in every library of the kingdom, proclaiming our poor barrister a fool!

O, thou watchful scribe, forbear! for it is cowardly—they

cannot smite again: forbear! for it is cruel—the hearts of wife and mother and lover ache upon your idle words: forbear! it is unreasonable—for often-times a word would prove that Rhadamanthus' self is wrong: forbear, calumnious scribe! and heed the harms you do, when you rob some poor struggler of his character for sense, and make the bread of the hungry to fail.

'*The Corinthian*,' another snarling watch-dog in the courts of the temple of Fame, followed instinctively the same injurious wake: it was a leisurely sarcastic anatomization, quite enough to blight any young candidate's prospects, supposing that mankind respected such a verdict; if not to make him cut his throat, granting that the victim should be sensitive as Keats. The generous review in question may be judged of by its first line and last sentence; as Hercules from his advancing foot, or Cuvier's Megatherium from the relics of its great toe. Thus it commenced:

"When a disappointed man, intolerant of fortune," &c., &c., and it wound up many stinging observations with this grateful climax following:

"We trust we have now said enough to prove that if a man will be bold enough to 'depreciate censure,'—will attack what he is pleased to consider abuses, however countenanced by high authority—and will obtrude his literary eloquence into our solemn courts of law, he deserves— what does he not deserve?—to be addressed henceforth by a name suggestive at once of ignorance, presumption, and conceit, as Mr. Henry Clements."

Now, will it be believed that a trivial error of the press mainly conduced to occasion this hostility? Our poor author had been weak enough to "deprecate censure" in his penny-wise humility, and the printer had negatived his meaning as above: "*hinc illæ lachrymæ.*" Oh, but how the ragged tooth of calumny gnawed his very heart!

'*The Legal Recorder*' was another of those early unfavourables; being as a matter of course adverse too, and not very disinterestedly either: for it played the exalted part of pet puffer to a rival publisher, who wanted no other reason for condemning this book of Mr. Clements than that it came from the legal officina of an opponent in his trade. There was another paper or two, but Clements felt so utterly disheartened that he did not dare to look at them. I wish he had; they would have comforted him, pouring balm upon his wounded pride by their kind and cordial praises: but ill-luck ruled the hour, so he burnt them forthwith, and lost much literary comforting.

To sauce up all this pleasantry with a smack of concreted pleasure itself, the last and only remaining document upon the table was a civil note from Mr. Wormwood, publisher and bookseller, enclosing the following items with his compliments:

To 500 copies '*Doctrine of Defence*,'	£124 3
To advertising ditto,	25 0
To 10 per cent. on sales,	&c.
Supplied to author, 12 copies,	&c.
Given to periodicals for review, 15 copies,	&c.

Against all which was the solitary offset of "three copies sold;" leaving as our Henry's *share* of now certain loss a matter of eighty pounds: which, between ourselves, was only a very little more than the whole cost of that untoward publication. Mr. Wormwood hoped to hear from Mr. Clements at his earliest convenience, as a certain sum was to be made up on a certain day, and the book-trade never had been at a lower ebb, and prompt payment would be esteemed a great accommodation, and—all that stereotyped sort of thing.

Poor Clements—reviled author, ruined lawyer, almost reckless wight—here was an extinguisher indeed to the morning's brilliant hopes! What an overwhelming debt to that ill-used couple in their altered circumstances! How entirely by his own strong effort had he swamped his legal expectations! Just as a man who cannot swim splashes himself into certain suffocation; whereas, if he would but lie quite still, he was certain to have floated on as safe as cork.

Well: to cut a long story short, our unlucky author found that he must pay, and pay forthwith, or incur a lawyer's bill for his debt to Mr. Wormwood: so he gave up his Temple garret, sold his books, nicknacks, and superfluous habiliments, added to the proceeds their forty pounds of capital, and a neck-chain of Maria's; and, at tremendous sacrifices, found himself once more out of danger, because out of debt. But it was a bad prospect truly for the future—ay, and for the present too; a few pounds left would soon be gone—and then dear Maria's confinement was approaching, and a hundred wants and needs, little and great: accordingly, they made all haste to get rid of their suburban dwelling in the City Road, collected their few valuables remaining, and retreated with all economical speed to a humble lodging in a cheap back street at Islington.

That little parlor was a palace of love: in the midst of her deep sorrow, sweet Maria never failed of her amiable charities—nay, she was even cheerful, hopeful—happy, and rendering happy: a thousand times a day had Henry cause to bless his "wedded angel." And, showing his love by more than words, he resolutely set about another literary enterprise, anonymous this time for very fear's sake; but Providence saw fit to bless his efforts with success. He wrote

Martin Farquhar Tupper

a tragedy, a clever and a good one too; though '*The Watchman*' did sneer about "modern Shakspeares," and '*The Corinthian*,' pouncing on some trifling fault, pounded it with would-be giant force: nevertheless, for it was a famous English theme, he luckily got them to accept it at the Haymarket, and '*Boadicea*' drew full houses; so the author had his due ninth night, and pocketed, instead of fame (for he grimly kept his secret) enough to enable him to print his tragedy for private satisfaction; and that piece of vanity accomplished, he still found himself seven pounds beforehand with the world.

CHAPTER XI

FRAUD CUTS HIS FINGERS WITH HIS OWN EDGED TOOLS

Unpleasant as it is to feel obliged to be the usher of ill company, I must now introduce to the fastidious public a brace of characters any thing but reputable. It were possible indeed to slur them over with a word; but I have deeper ends in view for a glance so superficial: we may learn a lesson in charity, we may gain some schooling of the heart, even from those "ladies-legatees."

Do you remember them, the supposititious nieces, aiders and abetters in our stock-jobber's forged will? Two flashy, showy women, *not* of easy virtue, but of none at all—special intimates of John Dillaway, and the genus of his like, and habitual frequenters of divers choice and pleasant places of resort.

The reason of their introduction here is two-fold: first, they have to play a part in our tale—a part of righteous retribution; and, secondly, they have to instruct us incidentally in this lesson of true morals and human charity—dread, denounce, and hate the sin, but feel a just compassion for the sinner. Let us take the latter object first, and bear with the brief epitome of facts which have blighted those unfortunates to what they are.

Look at these two women, impudent brawlers, foul with vice: can there be any excuses made for them, considered as distinct from their condition? God knoweth: listen to their histories; and fear not that thy virtuous glance will be harmed or misdirected, or a minute of thy precious time ill-spent.

Anna Bates and Julia Manners (their latest *noms de guerre* will serve all nominative purposes as well as any other) had arrived at the same lowest level of female degradation by very different downward roads. Anna's father had been a country curate, unfortunate through life, because utterly imprudent, and neither too wise a man nor too good a one, or depend upon it his orphan could not have come to this: "Never saw I the righteous forsaken, nor his seed begging their bread." But the father died carelessly as he had lived—in debt, with all his little affairs at sixes and sevens; and his widow with her budding daughter, saving almost nothing from the wreck, set up for milliners at Hull. Then did the mother pique herself upon playing her cards cleverly; for gallant Captain Croker was quite smitten with the girl. Poor child—she loved, listened, and was lost; a more systematic traitor of affection never breathed than that fine man; so she left by night her soft intriguing broken-spirited mother, followed her Lothario from barrack to barrack, and at last—he flung her away! Who can wonder at the reckless and dissolute result? Whom had she to care for her—whom had she to love? She must live thus, or starve. Without credit, character, or hope, or help, the friendless unprotected wretch was thrown upon the town. When the last accounts are opened, oblivious General Croker will find an ell-long score of crimes laid to his charge, whereof he little reckons in his sear and yellow leaf. The trusting victim of seduction has a legion of excuses for the wretched one she is.

Again; for another case whereon the better-favoured heart may ruminate in charity. Miss Julia Manners had a totally different experience but man can little judge how mainly the iron hand of circumstance confined that life-long sinner to the ways and works of guilt. In the nervous language of the Bible—(hear it, men and women, without shrinking from the words)—that poor girl was "the seed of the adulterer and the whore:" born in a brothel, amongst outcasts from a better mass of life—brought up from the very cradle amid sounds and scenes of utter vice (whereof we dare not think or speak one moment of the many years she dwelt continuously among them)—educated solely as a profligate, and ignorant alike of sin, righteousness, and a judgment to come—had she then a chance of good, or one hopeful thought of being better than she was? The water of holy baptism never bedewed that brow; the voice of motherly counsel never touched those ears; her eyes were unskilled to read the records of wisdom; her feet untutored to follow after holiness; her heart unconscious of those evils which she never knew condemned; her soul—she never heard or thought of one! Oh, ye well-born, well-bred, ye kindly, carefully, prayerfully instructed daughters of innocence and purity, pause, pause, ere your charity condemns: hate the sin, but love the sinner: think it out further, for yourselves, in all those details which I have not time to touch, skill to describe, nor courage to encounter; think out as kindly as ye may this episode of just indulgence; there is wisdom in this lesson of benevolence, and after-sweetness too, though the earliest taste of it be bitter; think it out; be humbler of your virtue, scarcely competent to err; be more grateful to that Providence which hath filled your lot with good; and be gentler-hearted, more generous-handed unto those whose daily life is—all temptation.

Now, these two ladies (who extenuates their guilt, caviller? who breathes one iota of excuse for their wicked manner of life? who does not utterly denounce the foul and flagrant sin, whilst he leaves to a secret-searching God the judgment of the sinner?)—these two ladies, I say, had of late become very sore plagues to Mr. John Dillaway. They had flared out their hush-money like duchesses, till the whole town rang about their equipage and style; and now, that all was spent, they pestered our stock-jobber for more. They came at an unlucky season, a season of "ill luck!" such a miraculous run of it, as nothing could explain to any rational mind but loaded dice, packed cards, contrivance and conspiracy. Nevertheless, our worthy John went on staking, and betting, and playing, resolute to break the bank, until it was no wonder at all to any but his own shrewd genius, that he found himself one feverish morning well nigh penniless. At such a moment then, called our ladies-legatees, clamorous for hush-money.

As a matter most imperatively of course, not a farthing more should be forthcoming, and many oaths avouched that stern determination. They ought to be ashamed of themselves, after such an enormous bribe to each—as if shame of any kind had part or lot in those feminine accomplices: it was a sanguine thought of Mr. John Dillaway. But the ladies were not ashamed, nor silenced, nor any thing like satisfied. So, having thoroughly fatigued themselves with out-swearing and out-threatening, our sneerful stock-jobber, they resolved upon exposing him, come what might. For their own guilty part in that transaction of Mrs. Jane Mackenzie's pseudo-will, good sooth, the wretched women had no characters to lose, nor scarcely aught else on which one could set a value. Danger and the trial would be an excitement to their pallid spirits, possible transportation even seemed a ray of hope, since any thing was better than the town; and in their sinful recklessness, liberty or life itself was little higher looked on than a dice's stake. Moreover, as to all manner of personal pains and penalties, there was every chance of getting off scot-free, provided they lost no time, went not one before the other, but doubly turned queen's evidence at once against their worthy coadjutor and employer. In the hope, then, of ruining him, if not of getting scathelessly off themselves, these ladies-legatees mustered once more from the mazes of St. Giles's the pack of competent Irish witnesses, collected whatever documentary or other evidence looked likeliest to help their ends, and then one early day presented themselves before the lord-mayor, eager to destroy at a blow that pleasant Mr. Dillaway.

The proceedings were long, cautious, tedious, and secret: emissaries to Belfast, Doctors' Commons, and the bank: the stamp office was stirred to its foundations; and Canterbury staggered at the fraud. Thus within a week the proper officials were in a condition to prosecute, and the issue of immense examinations tended to that point of satisfaction, the haling Mr. Dillaway to prison on the charge of having forged a will.

CHAPTER XII

HEART'S CORE

They were come into great want, poor Henry and Maria: they had not wherewithal for daily sustenance. The few remaining trinkets, books, clothes, and other available moveables had been gradually pledged away, and to their full amount—at least, the pawnbroker said so. That unlucky publication of the law book, so speedily condemned and heartlessly ridiculed, had wrecked all Henry's possible prospects in the courts; and as for help from friends—the casual friends of common life—he was too proud to beg for that—too sensitive, too self-respectful. Relations he had none, or next to none—that distant cousin of his mother's, the Mac-some-thing, whom he had never even seen, but who, nevertheless, had acted as his guardian.

Much as he suspected Dillaway in the matter of that bitter breach of trust, he had neither ready money to proceed against him, (nor, when he came to think it over) any legal grounds at all to go upon; for, as we have said before, even granting there should be evidence adduced of the transfer of stock from the name of Clements to that of Dillaway, still it was a notorious fact that the "Independent bank" had failed, whereto the stock-broker could swear he had intrusted it. In short, shrewd Jack had managed all that affair to admiration;

and poor Clements was ruined without hope, and defrauded without remedy.

Then, again, we already know how that Lady Dillaway was dead, so help from her was simply impossible; and the miserable father Sir Thomas was kept too closely up to the mark of resolute anger by slanderous John, to give them any aid, if they applied to him; but, in truth, as to personal application, Henry would not for pride, and Maria now could not, for her near-at-hand motherly condition. Her frequent letters, as we may be sure, were intercepted; and, even if Sir Thomas now and then yearned after his lost child, it had become a matter of physical impossibility to find out where she lived. Thus were they hopelessly sinking, day by day, into all the bitter waves of want. Not but that Henry strived, as we have seen, and shall yet see: still his endeavours had been very nearly fruitless—and, perchance, till all available moveables had been pawned outright, very feeble too. Now, however, that Maria, in her sorrow and her need, must soon become a mother, the state of things grew terrible indeed; their horizon was all over black with clouds.

No: not all over. There is light under the darkness, a growing light that shall dispel the darkness; a precious light upon their souls, the early dawn of Heaven's eternal day; God's final end in all their troubles, the reaping-time of joy for their sowing-time of tears.

Without cant, affectation, or hypocrisy, there is but one panacea for the bruised or broken heart, available alike in all times, all places, and all circumstances: and he who knows not what that is, has more to learn than I can teach him. That pure substantial comfort is born of Heaven's hope, and faith in Heaven's wisdom; it is a solid confidence in God's great love, but faintly shadowed out by all the charities of earth. Human affections in their manifold varieties are little other

Martin Farquhar Tupper

than an echo of that Voice, "Come unto me; Comfort ye, comfort ye; I will be a Father unto you, and ye shall be my sons and my daughters; thy Maker is thy Husband; he hath loved thee with an everlasting love; when thou goest through the fire, I will be with thee, through the waters, they shall not overflow thee; eye hath not seen, nor ear heard, neither hath it entered into the mind of man to conceive the blessings which His love hath laid in store for *thee*."

Heart's-ease in heart's-affliction—this they found in God; turning to Him with all their hearts, and pouring out their hearts before Him, they trusted in Him heartily for both worlds' good. Therefore did He give them their heart's desire, satisfying all their mind: wherefore did they love each other now with a newly-added plenitude of love, mutually in reference to Him who loved them, and gave Himself for them: therefore did they feel in their distresses more gladness at their hearts, than in the days of luxury and affluence, the increase of their oil and their wine.

For this is the great end of all calamities. God doth not willingly afflict: trouble never cometh without an urgent cause; and though man in his perverseness often misses all the prize of purity, whilst he pays all the penalty of pain; still the motive that sent sorrow was the same—O, that there were a better heart in them!

In many modes the heart of man is tried, as gold must be refined, by many methods; and happiest is the heart, that, being tried by many, comes purest out of all. If prosperity melts it as a flux, well; but better too than well, if the acid of affliction afterwards eats away all unseen impurities; whereas, to those with whom the world is in their hearts, affluence only hardens, and penury embitters, and thus, though burnt in many fires, their hearts are dross in all. Like those sullen children in the market-place, they feel no sympathies with heaven or with earth: unthankful in prosperity, unsoftened by adversity, well may it be said of them, Hearts of stone, hearts of stone!

Not of such were Henry and Maria: naturally warm in affections and generous in sympathies, it needed but the pilot's hand to steer their hearts aright: the energies of life were there, both fresh and full, lacking but direction heavenwards; and chastisement wisely interposed to wean those yearning spirits from the brief and feverish pursuits of unsatisfying life, to the rest and the rewards of an eternity. Then were they wedded indeed, heart answering to heart; then were they strong against all the ills of life, those hearts that were established by grace; then spake they often one to another out of the abundance of their hearts; and in spite of all their sorrows, they were happy, for their hearts were right with God.

Let the grand idea suffice, unencumbered by the multitude of details. Whatsoever things are true, honest and just; whatsoever things are pure, lovely, or of good report; if there be any virtue, and if there be any praise—believe of those twin hearts that God had given them all. Patience, hope, humility; faith, tenderness, and charity; prayer, trust, benevolence, and joy: this was the lot of the afflicted! It was good for them that they had been in trouble; for they had gained from it a wealth that is above the preciousness of rubies, deservedly dearer to their hearts than the thousands of gold and silver.

What a contrast then was shown between God's kindness and man's coldness! No one of their fellows seemed to give them any heed: but He cared for them, and on Him they cast their cares. Former friends appeared to stand aloof, self-dependent and unsympathizing; but God was ever near, kindly bringing help in every extremity, which always seemed at hand, yet ever kept away: smoothing the pillow of sickness, comforting the troubled spirit, and treading down calamity and calumny and care; as a conqueror conquering for them. So, they learned the priceless wisdom which adversity would teach to all on whom she frowneth; when earthly hopes are wrecked, to anchor fast on God; and if affluence should ever come again, to aid the poor afflicted with heartiness, beneficence, and home-taught sympathy.

CHAPTER XIII

HOPE'S BIRTH TO INNOCENCE,
AND HOPE'S DEATH TO FRAUD

John Dillaway's sudden loss of property, his character exploded as a monied man, and the strong probability of his turning out a felon, had a great effect on the spirits of Sir Thomas. He had called upon his promising son in prison, had found him very sulky, disinclined for social intercourse, and any thing but filial; all he condescended to growl, with a characteristic d—or two interlarding his eloquence, was this taunting speech:

"Well, governor, I may thank you and your counsels for this. Here's a precious end to all my clever tricks of trade! I wish you joy of your son, and of your daughter too, old man. Who wrote that letter? What, not found out yet? and does she still starve for it? Who gained money as you bade him—never mind how? And is now going to do honour to the family all round the world, ey?—Ha, ha, ha!"

The poor unhappy father tottered away as quickly as he could, while yet the brutal laughter of that unnatural son rang upon his ears. He was quite miserable, let him turn which way he would. On 'Change the name had been disgraced— posted up for scorn on the board of degradation: at home, there was no pliant son and heir, to testify against Maria, and to close the many portals of a wretched father's heart. He grew very wretched—very mopy; determined upon cutting adrift shrewd Jack himself, as a stigma on the name which had once held the mace of mayoralty; made his will petulantly, for good and all, in favour of Stationer's hall, and felt very like a man who had lived in vain. "Cut it down; why cumbereth it the earth?"

Meanwhile, in those two opposite quarters of the world of London, Newgate and Islington, Sir Thomas's two discarded children were bearing in a different way their different privations. Poor Maria's hour of peril had arrived; and amidst all those pains, dangers, and necessities, a soft and smiling babe was born into the world; gladness filled their hearts, and praise was on their tongues, when the happy father and mother kissed that first-born son. It was a splendid boy, they said, and should redeem his father's fortunes: there was hope in the future, let the past be what it may; and this new bond of union to that happy wedded pair made the present—one unclouded scene of gratitude and love. Who shall sing of the humble ale-caudle, and those cheerful givings to surrounding poor, scarcely poorer than themselves? Who shall record how kind was Henry, how useful was the nurse, how liberal the doctor, how sympathizing all? Who shall tell how tenderly did Providence step in with another author's night of that same tragedy, and how other avenues to literary gain stood wide open to industry and genius? It was happiness all, happiness, and triumph: they were weathering the storm famously, and had safely passed the breakers of False witness.

Amidst the other part of London sate a sullen fellow, quite alone, in Newgate, looking for his trial on the morrow, and prophesying accurately enough how some two days hence, he, John Dillaway, of Broker's alley, son and heir of the richest stationer in Europe, was to appear in the character of a convicted felon, and be probably condemned to transportation for life. A pleasant retrospect was his, a pleasanter aspect, and a pleasanter prospect; all was pleasure assuredly.

And the morrow duly came; with those implacable approvers, those accurate Irish witnesses, those tell-tale documents, that prosecuting crown and bank, that dogged jury, and that sentencing recorder: so then, by a little after noon, to the scandal of Finsbury square, John Dillaway discovered that the "wise man's trick or two in the money market" was about to be rewarded with twenty-one years of transportation.

Of this interesting fact Henry Clements became acquainted by an occasional peep into the public prints; and he perceived to his astonishment, that the defrauded Mrs. Jane Mackenzie, of Ballyriggan, near Belfast, could surely be none other than his mother's Ulster cousin, the nominal guardian of his boyhood! To be sure, it mattered little enough to him, for the old lady had never been much better than a stranger to him, and at present appeared only in that useless character to an expectant, a person despoiled of her money; nevertheless, of that identical money, certain sanguine friends had heretofore given him expectations in the event of her death, seeing that she had nobody to leave it to, except himself and the public charities of the United Kingdom: clearly, this cousin must have been the defrauded bank annuitant, and he could not help feeling more desolate than ever; for John Dillaway's evil influences had robbed him now of name, fame, fortune, and what hope regards as much as any—expectations. Yet—must not the bank of England bear the brunt of all this forgery, and account for its stock to that innocent depositor? Old Mrs. Jane was sinking into dotage, probably had plenty of other money, and scarcely seemed to stir about the business; therefore, legitimately interested as Henry indubitably was, he took upon him to write to his antiquated relative, and in so doing managed to please her mightily: renewed whatever interest she ever might have felt in him, enabled her to enforce her just claim, and really stood a likelier chance than ever of coming in for competency some day. However, for the present, all was penury still. Clements had been too delicate for even a hint at his deplorable condition: and his distant relative's good feeling, so providentially renewed, served indeed to gild the future, but did not avail to gingerbread the present. So they struggled on as well as they could: both very thankful for the chance which had caused a coalition between sensitiveness and interest; and Maria at least more anxious than ever for a reconciliation with her father, now that all his ardent hopes had been exploded in son John.

CHAPTER XIV

PROBABLE RECONCILIATION

It was no use—none at all. Nature was too strong for him; and a higher force than even potent Nature. In vain Sir Thomas pish'd, and tush'd, and bah'd; in vain he buried himself chin-deep amongst the century of ledgers that testified of gainful years gone by, and were now mustily rotting away in the stagnant air of St. Benet's Sherehog: interest had lost its interest for him, profits profited not, speculation's self had dull, lack-lustre eyes, and all the hard realities of utilitarian life were become weary, flat, and stale. Sir Thomas was a miserable man—a bereaved old man— who nevertheless clung to what was left, and struggled not to grieve for what was lost: there was a terrible strife going on secretly within him, dragging him this way and that: a little, lightning flash of good had been darted by Omnipotence right through the stone-built caverns of his heart, and was smouldering a concentred flame within its innermost hollow; a small soft-skinned seed had been dropped by the Father of Spirits into that iron-bound soil, and it was swelling day by day under the case-hardened surface, gradually with gentle violence, despite of all the locks and gates, and bolts and bars, a silent enemy had somehow crept within the fortress of his feelings, ready at any unguarded moment to fling the portals open. The rock had a sealed fountain leaping within it, as an infant in the womb. The poor old man, the worldly cold old man, was giving way.

Happy misery! for his breaking heart revealed a glorious jewel at the core. Oh, sorrow beyond price! for natural affections, bursting up amid these unsunned snows, were a hot-spring to that Iceland soul. Oh, bitter, bitter penitence most blest! which broke down the money-proud man, which bruised and kneaded him, humbled, smote, and softened him, and made him come again a little child—a loving, yearning, little child—a child with pity in its eyes, with prayer upon its tongue, with generous affection in its heart. "Oh, Maria! precious, cast-off child, where art thou, where art thou, where art thou—starving? And canst thou, blessed God, forgive? And will not thy great mercy bring her to me yet again? Oh, what a treasury of love have I mis-spent; what riches of the Heart, what only truest wealth, have I, poor prodigal, been squandering! Unhappy son—unhappy father of the perjured, heartless, miserable John! Wo is me! Where art thou, dear child, my pure and best Maria?"

We may well guess, far too well, how it was that dear Maria came not near him. She had been, prior to confinement, very, very ill: nigh to death: the pangs of travail threatened to have seized upon her all too soon, when wasted with sorrow, and weakened by want. She lay, long weeks, battling for life, in her little back parlour, at Islington, tended night and day by her kind, good husband.

But did she not often (you will say) urge him, earnestly as the dying ask, to seek out her father or brother (she had not been told of his conviction), and to let them know this need? Why, then, did he so often put her off with faint excuses, and calm her with coming hopes, and do any thing, say any thing, suffer any thing, rather than execute the fervent wish of the affectionate Maria? It is easily understood. With, and notwithstanding, all the high sentiments, strong sense, and warm feelings of Henry Clements, he was too proud to seek any succour of the Dillaways. Sooner than give that hard old man, or, beforetime, that keen malicious young one, any occasion to triumph over his necessitous condition, he himself would starve: ay, and trust to Heaven his darling wife and child; but not trust these to them. Never, never—if the heart-divorcing work-house were their doom—should that father or that brother hear from him a word of supplication, or one murmur of complaint. Nay; he took pains to hinder their knowledge of this trouble: all the world, rather than those two men. Let penury, disease, the very parish-beadle triumph over him, but not those two. It was a natural feeling for a sensitive mind like his—but in many respects a wrong one. It was to put away, deliberately, the helping hand of Providence, because it bade him kiss the rod. It was a direct preference of honour to humility. It was an unconsciously unkind consideration of himself before those whom he nevertheless believed and called more dear to him than life—but not than honour. Therefore it was that the hand-bills he had so often seen pasted upon walls were disregarded, that the numerous newspaper advertisements remained unanswered, and that all the efforts of an almost frantic father to find his long-lost daughter were in vain.

Meanwhile, to be just upon poor Clements, who really fancied he was doing right in this, he left no stone unturned to obtain a provision for his beloved wife and child. Frequently, by letters (as little urgent as affection and necessity would suffer him), he had pressed upon some powerful friends for that vague phantom of a gentlemanly livelihood—"something under government;" a hope improbable of accomplishment, indefinite as to view, but still a hope: especially, since very civil answers came to his request, couched in terms of official guardedness. He had called anxiously upon "old friends," in pretty much of his usual elegant dress (for he was wise enough, or proud enough, never to let his poverty be seen in his attire), and they made many polite inquiries after "Mrs. Clements," and "Where are you living?" and "How is it you never come our way?" and "Clements has cut us all dead," and so forth. It was really entirely his own fault, but he never could contrive to tell the truth: and when one day, in a careless tone of voice, he threw out something about "Do you happen to have ten pounds about you?" to a dashing young blood of his acquaintance—the dashing young blood affected to treat it as a joke—"You married men, lucky dogs, with your regular establishments, are too hard upon us poor bachelors, who have nothing but clubs to go to. I give you my honour, Clements, ten pounds would dine me for a fortnight:—spare me this time, there's a fine fellow: take the trouble to write a cheque on your bankers—here's paper—and my tiger shall get it cashed for you while you wait: we poor bachelors are never flush." But Clements had already owned it was a mere "*obiter dictum*,"—nothing but a joke of prudent marriage against extravagant bachelorship.

Ah, what a bitter joke was that! On the verge of that yes or no, to be uttered by his frank young friend, trembled reluctant honour; home-affections were imploring in that careless tone of voice; hunger put that off-hand question. It was vain; a cruel killing effort for his pride: so Henry Clements never asked again; withdrew himself from friends; grew hopeless, all but reckless; and his only means of living were picked up scantily from the by-ways of literature. An occasional guinea from a magazine, a copy of that luckily anonymous tragedy now and then sold by him from house to house (he always disguised himself at such times), a little indexing to be done for publishers, and a little correcting of the press for printers—these formed the trifling and uncertain pittance upon which the pale family existed. Poor Henry Clements, proud Henry Clements, you had, indeed, a dose of physic for your pride: bitter draughts, bitter draughts, day after day; but, for all that weak and wasted wife, dearly, devotedly beloved; for all the pining infant, with its angel face and beautiful smiles: for all the strong pleadings of affection, yea, and gnawing hunger too, the strong man's pride was stronger. And had not God's good providence proved mercifully strongest of them all, that family of love would have starved outright for pride.

But Heaven's favour willed it otherwise. By something little short of miracle, where food was scant and medicine scarce, the poor emaciated mother gradually gained strength—that long, low fever left her, health came again upon her cheek, her travail passed over prosperously, the baby too thrived, (oh, more than health to mothers!) and Maria Clements found herself one morning strong enough to execute a purpose she had long most anxiously designed. "Henry was wrong to think so harshly of her father. She knew he would not spurn her away: he must be kind, for she loved him dearly still. Wicked as it doubtless was of her [dear innocent girl] to have done any thing contrary to his wishes, she was sure he would relieve her in her utmost need. He could not, could not be so hard as poor dear Henry made him." So, taking advantage of her husband's absence during one of his literary pilgrimages, she took her long-forgotten bonnet and shawl, and, with the baby in her arms, flew on the wings of love, duty, penitence, and affection to her dear old home in Finsbury square.

Martin Farquhar Tupper

CHAPTER XV

THE FATHER FINDS HIS HEART FOR EVER

He had been at death's door, sinking out of life, because he had nothing now to live for. He still was very weak in bed, faint, and worn, and white, propped up with pillows—that poor, bereaved old man. Ever since Lady Dillaway's most quiet death he had felt alone in the world. True, while she lived she had seemed to him a mere tranquil trouble, a useless complacent piece of furniture, often in his way; but now that she was dead, what a void was left where she had been—mere empty space, cold and death-like. She had left him quite alone.

Then again—of John, poor John, he would think, and think continually—not about the little vulgar pock-marked man of 'change, the broker, the rogue, the coward—but of a happy curly child, with sparkling eyes—a merry-hearted, ruddy little fellow, romping with his sister—ay, in this very room; here is the identical China vase he broke, all riveted up; there is the corner where he would persist to nestle his dormice. Ah, dear child! precious child! where is he now?—Where and what indeed! Alas, poor father! had you known what I do, and shall soon inform the world, of that bad man's awful end, one more, one fiercest pang would have tormented you: but Heaven spared that pang. Nevertheless, the bitter contrast of the child and of the man had made him very wretched—and to the widower's solitude added the father's sadness.

And worst of all—Maria's utter loss—that dear, warm-hearted, innocent, ill-used, and yet beloved daughter. Why did he spurn her away? and keep her away so long?—oh, hard heart, hard heart! Was she not innocent, after all? and John, bad John, too probably the forger of that letter, as the forger of this will? And now that he should give his life to see her, and kiss her, and—no, no, not forgive her, but pray to be forgiven by her—"Where is she? why doesn't she come to hold up my poor weak head—to see how fervently my dead old heart has at last learnt to love—to help a bad, and hard, a pardoned and penitent old man to die in perfect peace—to pray with me, for me, to God, our God, my daughter! Where is she—how can I find her out—why will she not come to me all this sorrowful year? Oh come, come, dear child—our Father send thee to me—come and bless me ere I die—come, my Maria!"

Magical, or contrived, as it may seem to us, the poor old man was actually bemoaning himself thus, when our dear heroine of the Heart faintly knocked at her old home door. It opened; a faded-looking woman, with a baby in her arms, rushed past the astonished butler: and, just as her father was praying out aloud for Heaven to speed her to him, that daughter's step was at the bed-room door.

Before she turned the handle (some house-maid had recognised her on the stairs, and told her, with an impudent air, that "Sir Thomas was ill a-bed"), she stopped one calming instant to gain strength of God for that dreaded interview, and to check herself from bursting in upon the chamber of sickness, so as to disquiet that dear weak patient. So, she prayed, gently turned the handle, and heard those thrilling words—"Come, my Maria!"

It was enough; their hearts burst out together like twin fountains, rolling their joyful sorrows together towards the sea of endless love, as a swollen river that has broken through some envious and constraining dam! It was enough; they wept together, rejoiced together, kissed and clasped each other in the fervour of full love: the babe lay smiling and playing on the bed: Maria, in a torrent of happiest tears, fondled that poor old man, who was crying and laughing by turns, as little children do—was praising God out loud like a saint, and calling down blessings on his daughter's head in all the transports of a new-found Heart. What a world of things they had to tell of—how much to explain, excuse, forgive, and be forgiven, especially about that wicked letter—how fervently to make up now for love that long lay dormant— how heartily to bless each other, and to bless again! Who can record it all? Who can even sketch aright the heavenly hues that shone about that scene of the affections? Alas, my pen is powerless—yea, no mortal hand can trace those heavenly hues. Angels that are round the penitent's, the good man's bed—ye alone who witness it, can utter what ye see: ye alone, rejoicingly with those rejoicing, gladly speed aloft frequent ambassadors to Him, the Lord of Love, with some new beauteous trait, some rare ecstatic thought, some pure delighted look, some more burning prayer, some gem of Heaven's jewellery more brilliant than the rest, which raises happy envy of your bright compeers. I see your shining bands crowding enamoured round that scene of human tenderness; while now and then some peri-like seraph of your thronging spiritual forms will gladly wing away to find favour of his God for a tear, or a prayer, or a holy thought dropped by his ministering hands into the treasury of Heaven.

But the cup of joy is large and deep: it is an ocean in capacity: and mantling though it seemeth to the brim, God's bounty poureth on.

Another step is on the stairs! You have guessed it, Henry Clements. Returning home wearily, after a disheartening expedition, and finding his wife, to his great surprise, gone out, sick and weak, as still he thought her, he had calculated justly on the direction whereunto her heart had carried her; he had followed her speedily, and, with many self-compunctions, he had determined to be proud no more, and to help, with all his heart, in that holy reconciliation. See! at the bedside, folding Maria with one arm, and with his other hand tightly clasped in both of that kind and changed old man's, stands Henry Clements.

Ay, changed indeed! Who could have discovered in that joy-illumined brow, in those blessing-dropping lips, in those eyes full of penitence, and pity, and peace, and praise, and prayer, the harsh old usurer—the crafty money-cankered knave of dim St. Benet's Sherehog—the cold husband—the cruel father—the man without a heart? Ay, changed—changed for ever now, an ever of increasing happiness and love. Who or what had caused this deep and mighty change? Natural affection was the sword, and God's the arm that wielded it. None but he could smite so deeply; and when he smote, pour balm into the wound: none but He could kill death, that dead dried heart, and quicken life within its mummied caverns: none but the Voice, which said "Let there be light," could work this common miracle of "Let there be love."

He grew feebler—feebler, that dying kind old man: it had been too much for him, doubtlessly; he had long been ill, and should long ago have died; but that he had lived for this; and now the end seemed near. They never left his bed-side then for days and nights, that new-found son and daughter: physicians came, and recommended that the knight be quite alone, quite undisturbed: but Sir Thomas would not, could not—it were cruelty to force it; so he lay feebly on his back, holding on either side the hands of Henry and Maria.

It was not so very long: they had come almost in the nick of time: a few days and hours at the most, and all will then be over. So did they watch and pray.

And the old man faintly whispered:

"Henry—son Henry: poor John, forgive him, as you and our God have now forgiven me; poor John—when he comes back again from those long years of slavery, give him a home, son—give him a home, and enough to keep him honest; tell him I love him, and forgive him; and remind him that I died, praying Heaven for my poor boy's soul.

"Henry and Maria—I had, since my great distresses, well nigh forgotten this world's wealth; but now, thank God, I have thought of it all for your sakes: in my worst estate of mind I made a wicked will. It is in that drawer—quick, give it me.

"Thanks—thanks—there is time to tear it; and these good friends, Dr. Jones and Mr. Blair, take witness—I destroy this wicked will; and my only child, Maria, has my wealth in course of law. Wealth, yes—if well used, let us call it wealth; for riches may indeed be made a mine of good, and joy, and righteousness. I am unworthy to use any of it well, unworthy of the work, unworthy of the reward: use it well, my holier children, wisely, liberally, kindly: God give you to do great good with it; God give you to feel great happiness in all your doing good. My hands that saved and scraped it all, also often-times by evil hardness, now penitently washed in the Fountain of Salvation, heartily renounce that evil. Be ye my stewards; give liberally to many needy. Oh me, my sin! children, to my misery you know what need is: I can say no more; poor sinful man, how dare I preach to others?

Children, dearest ones, I am a father still; and I would bless you—bless you!

"I grow weak, but my heart seems within me to grow stronger—I go—I go, to the Home of Heart, where He that sits upon the throne is Love, and where all the pulses of all the beings there thrill in unison with him, the Great Heart of Heaven! I, even I, am one of the redeemed—my heart is fixed, I will sing and give praise; I, even I, the hardest and the worst, forgiven, accepted! Who are ye, bright messengers about my bed, heralds of glory? I go—I go—one—one more, Maria—one last kiss; we meet—again—in Heaven!"

Had he fainted? yes—his countenance looked lustrous, yet diminishing in glory, even as a setting sun; the living smile faded gradually away, and a tranquil cold calm crept over his cheeks: the angelic light which made his eyes so beautiful to look at, was going out—going out: all was peace—peace—deep peace.

O death, where is thy victory? O grave, where is thy sting?

CHAPTER XVI

A WORD ABOUT ORIGINALITY AND MOURNING

When a purely inventive genius concocts a fabulous tale, it is clearly competent to him so to order matters, that characters shall not die off till his book is shortly coming to an end: and had your obedient servant now been engaged in the architecture of a duly conventional story, arranged in pattern style, with climax in the middle and a brace of ups and downs to play supporters, doubtless he might easy have kept alive both father and mother to witness the triumph of innocence, and have produced their deaths at the last as a kind of "sweet sorrow," or honied sting, wherewithal to point his moral. Such, however, was not my authorship's intention; and, seeing that a wilful pen must have its way, I have chosen to construct my own veracious tale, respecting the incidents of life and death, much as such events not unfrequently occur, that is, at an inconvenient season: for though such accessories to the fact of dying, as triumphant conversion, or a tranquil going out, may appear to be a little out of the common way, still the circumstance of death itself often in real life seems to come as out of time, as your wisdom thinks in the present book of Heart. People will die untowardly, and people will live provokingly, notwith-standing all that novelists have said and poets sung to the contrary: and if two characters out of our principal five have already left the mimic scene, it will now be my duty only to show, as nature and society do, how, of those three surviving chief *dramatis personæ*, two of them—to wit, our hero and heroine of Heart—gathered many friends about their happy homestead, did a world of good, and, in fine, furnish our volume with a suitable counterpoise to the mass of selfish sin, which (at its height in the only remaining character) it has been my fortune to record and to condemn as the opposite topic of heartlessness.

If writers will be bound by classic rules, and walk on certain roads because other folks have gone that way before them, needs must that ill-starred originality perish from this world's surface, and find refuge (if it can) in the gentle moon or Sirius. Therefore, let us boldly trespass from the trodden paths, let us rather shake off the shackles of custom than hug them as an ornament approved: and, notwithstanding both parental deaths, seemingly ill-timed for the happiness of innocence, let us acquiesce in the facts, as plain matters of history, not dubious thoughts of fiction; and let us gather to the end any good we can, either from the miserable solitude of a selfish Dillaway, or from the hearty social circle of our happy married pair.

Need I, sons and daughters, need I record at any length how Maria mourned for her father? If you now have parents worthy of your love, if you now have hearts to love them, I may safely leave that theme to your affections: "now" is for all things "the accepted time," now is the day for reconciliations: our life is a perpetual now. However unfilial you may have been, however stern or negligent they, if there is now the will to bless, and now the heart to love, all is well— well at the last, well now for evermore—thank Heaven for so glad a consummation. Oh, that my pen had power to make many fathers kind, many children trustful! Oh, that by some burning word I could thaw the cold, shame sarcasms, and arouse the apathetic! Oh that, invoking upon every hearth, whereto this book may come, the full free blaze of home affections, my labour of love be any thing but vain, when God shall have blessed what I am writing!

Yes, children, dear Maria did mourn for her father, but she mourned as those who hope; his life had been forgiven, and his death was as a saints's: as for her, rich rewarded daughter at the last, one word of warm acknowledgement, one look of true affection, one tear of deep contrition, would have been superabundant to clear away all the many clouds, the many storms of her past home-life: and as for our Maker, with his pure and spotless justice, faith in the sacrifice had passed all sin to him, and love of the Redeemer had proved that faith the true one. How should a daughter mourn for such a soul? With tears of joy; with sighs—of kindred hopefulness; with happiest resolve to live as he had died; with instant prayer that her last end be like his.

There is a plain tablet in St. Benet's church, just within the altar-rail, bearing—no inscription about Lord Mayoralty, Knighthood, or the Worshipful Company of Stationers—but full of facts more glorious than every honour under heaven; for the words run thus:

SORROWFUL, YET REJOICING,
A DAUGHTER'S LOVE HAS PLACED THIS TABLET
TO THE MEMORY OF
T H O M A S D I L L A W A Y;
A MAN WHO DIED IN THE FAITH OF CHRIST,
IN THE LOVE OF GOD, AND IN THE HOPE OF
HEAVEN.

Noble epitaph! Let us so live, that the like of this may be truth on our tomb-stones. Seek it, rather than wealth, before honour, instead of pleasure; for, indeed, those words involve within their vast significancy riches unsearchable, glory indestructible, and pleasure for evermore! Hide them, as a string of precious pearls, within the casket of your hearts.

I had almost forgotten, though Maria never could, another neighbouring tablet to record the peaceful exit of her mother; however, as this had been erected by Sir Thomas in his life-time, and was plastered thick with civic glories and heathen virtues, possibly the transcript may be spared: there was only one sentence that looked true about the epitaph, though I wished it had been so in every sense; but, to common eyes, it had seemed quite suitable to the physical quietude of living Lady Dillaway, to say, "Her end was peace;" although, perhaps, the husband little thought how sore that mother's heart was for dear Maria's loss, how full of anxious doubts her mind about Maria's sin. Poor soul, however peaceful now that spirit has read the truth, in the hour of her departure it had been with her far otherwise: her dying bed was as a troubled sea, for she died of a broken heart.

Yearly, on the anniversaries of their respective deaths, the growing clan of Clements make a solemn pilgrimage to their grand paternal shrine, attending service on those days (or the holiday nearest to them), at St. Benet's Sherehog; and Maria's eyes are very moist on such occasions; though hope sings gladly too within her wise and cheerful heart. She does not seem to have lost those friends; they are only gone before.

CHAPTER XVII

THE HOUSE OF FEASTING

But in fact, with our happy married folks an anniversary of some sort is perpetually recurring: wedding-days, birth-days, and all manner of festival occasions, worthy (as the old Romans would have said) to be noted up with chalk, happened in that family of love weekly—almost daily. They cultivated well the grateful soil of Heart, by a thousand little dressings and diggings; courting to it the warm sunshine of the skies, the zephyrs of pleasant recollections, and the genial dews of sympathy. And very wise were all those labours of delight; for their sons and their daughters grew up as the polished corners in the temple; moulded with delicate affections, their moral essence sharp, and clearly edged with sensitive feelings, as if they had sprung fresh from the hands of God, their sculptor, and the world had not rubbed off the master-touches of His chisel. For, in this dull world, we cheat ourselves and one another of innocent pleasures by the score, through very carelessness and apathy: courted day after day by happy memories, we rudely brush them off with this indiscriminating bosom, the stern material present: invited to help in rendering joyful many a patient heart, we neglect the little word that might have done it, and continually defraud creation of its share of kindliness from us. The child made merrier by your interest in his toy; the old domestic flattered by your seeing him look so well; the poor, better helped by your blessing than your penny (though give the penny too); the labourer, cheered upon his toil by a timely word of praise; the humble friend encouraged by your frankness; equals made to love you by the expression of your love; and superiors gratified by attention and respect, and looking out to benefit the kindly—how many pleasures here for any hand to gather; how many blessings here for any heart to give! Instead of these, what have we rife about the world? Frigid compliment—for warmth is vulgar; reserve of tongue—for it is folly to be talkative; composure, never at fault—for feelings are dangerous things; gravity—for that looks wise; coldness—for other men are cold; selfishness—for every one is struggling for his own. This is all false, all bad; the slavery chain of custom riveted by the foolishness of fashion; because there ever is a band of men and women, who have nothing to recommend them but externals—their looks or their dresses, their rank or their wealth—and in order to exalt the honour of these, they agree to set a compact seal of silence on the heart and on the mind; lest the flood of humbler men's affections, or of wiser men's intelligence, should pale their tinsel-praise; and the warm and the wise too softly acquiesce in this injury done to heartiness shamed by the effrontery of cold calm fools, and the shallow dignity of an empty presence. Turn the tables on them, ye truer gentry, truer nobility, truer royalty of the heart and of the mind; speak freely, love warmly, laugh cheerfully, explain frankly, exhort zealously, admire liberally, advise earnestly—be not ashamed to show you have a heart: and if some cold-blooded simpleton greet your social effort with a sneer, repay him—for you can well afford a richer gift than his whole treasury possesses—repay him with a kind good-humoured smile: it would have shamed Jack Dillaway himself. If a man persists to be silent in a crowd for vanity's sake, instead of sociable, as good company expects, count him simply for a fool; you will not be far wrong; he remembers the copy-book at school, no doubt, with its large-text aphorism, "Silence is wisdom;" and thinking in an easy obedience to gain credit from mankind by acting on that questionable sentence, the result is what you perpetually see—a self-contained, self-satisfied, selfish, and reserved young puppy. Hint to such an incommunicative comrade, that the fashion now is coming about, to talk and show your wisdom; not to sit in shallow silence, hiding hard your folly; soon shall you loosen the flood-gates of his speech; and society will even thank you for it; for, bore as the chatterer may oft-times be, still he does the frank companion's duty; and at any rate is vastly preferable to the dull, unwarmed, unsympathetic watcher at the festal board, who sits there to exhibit his painted waistcoat instead of the heart that should be in it, and patiently waits, with a snakish eye and a bitter tongue, to aid conversation with a sarcasm.

Henry and Maria had many hearty friends to keep their many anniversaries. They were well enough for wealth, as we may guess without much trouble; for the knight had left three thousand a-year behind him, and Maria, as sole heiress, had no difficulty in establishing her claim to it; but it may be well to put mankind in memory how hospitably, how charitably, how wisely, and how heartily they stewarded it. I need not stop to tell of local charities assisted, good societies supported, and of philanthropic good done by means of their money, both at home and abroad: nor detail their many dinners, and other festal opportunities, rivets in the lengthening chain of ordinary friendship: but I do wish to make honourable mention of one happiest anniversary, which, while it commemorated fine young Master Harry's birth, rejoiced the many poor of Lower-Sack street, Islington.

The birth-day itself was kept at home with all the honours, in their old house at Finsbury square; Maria would not leave that house, for old acquaintance sake. Master Harry, a frank-faced, open-hearted, curly-headed boy of ten (at least when I dined there, for he has probably grown older since), was of course the happy hero of the feast, ably supported by divers joyful brothers and sisters, who had all contributed to their elder brother's triumph on that day, by the contribution of their various presents—one a little scent bag, another a rude drawing, another a book-marker, and so forth, all probably worthless in the view of selfish calculation, but inestimable according to the currency of Heart. Half-a-dozen choice old friends closed the list of company; and a noisy rout of boys and girls were added in the early evening, full of negus, and sponge-cake, snap-dragon, and blindman's-buff, with merry music, and a golden-flood of dances and delight.

We dined early; and, to be very confidential with you, I thought (until I found out reasons why), that the bill-of-fare upon the table was inordinately large, not to say vulgar; for the board was overloaded with solid sweets and savouries: so, in my uncharitable mind, I set all that down to the uncivilized hospitality asserted of a citizen's feast, and (for aught I know) still rife in St. Mary Axe and Finsbury square.

Never mind how the dinner passed off, nor how jovially the children kept it up till near eleven: for I learnt, in an incidental way, what was regularly done upon the morrow; and I am sure it will gratify my readers to learn it too, as a trait of considerate kindness which will gladden man and woman's heart.

On the seventh of April in every year (Harry's birth-day was the sixth), Henry and Maria used to go on an humble pilgrimage to Lower Sack street, Islington. Not to shame the poor by fine clothes or their usual equipage, they sedulously donned on that occasion the same now faded suits they had worn in their adversity, and made their progress in a hackney-coach. They would have walked for humility's sake and sympathy, but that the coach in question was crammed full of eatables and drinkables, nicely packed up in well-considered parcels, consisting of the vast *débris* of yesterday's overwhelming feast, with a sackful of tea and sugar added. Their pockets also, as I took the liberty of inquiring at Sack street afterwards, must have been well stored, for their largess was munificent. Then would they go to that identical lodgings of years gone by, where they had so struggled with adversity, now in the happy contrast of wealth and peace and thankfulness to Heaven, and of joy at doing good. That parlour was right liberally hired for the day, and all the poor in Sack street were privileged to call, where Mrs. Clements held her levee. They came in an orderly stream, clean for the occasion, and full of gratitude and blessings; and, to be just upon the poor, no impostor had ever been known to intrude upon the privilege of Sack street. As for dear Maria, she regularly broke down just as the proceedings commenced, and Henry's manlier hand had to give away the spoil; whilst Maria sobbed beside him, as if her heart would break. Then did the good old nurse come in for a cold round of beef, with tea, sugar, and a sovereign; and the bed-ridden neighbour up-stairs for jellied soup, and other condiments, with a similar royal climax; and the cobbler over the way carried off ham and chickens, with apple-puffs and a bottle of wine: and so some thirty or forty families were gladdened for the hour, and made wealthy for a week. Altogether they divided amongst them a coachful of comestibles, and a pocketful of coin.

It would be impertinent in us to intrude so far on privacy, as to record how Henry and Maria passed much time in prayer and praise on that interesting anniversary; it is unnecessary too, for in fact they did not stop for anniversaries to do that sort of thing. Be sure that good thoughts and good words are ever found preceding good and grateful deeds. It is quite enough to know that they did God service in doing good to man.

CHAPTER XVIII

THE END OF THE HEARTLESS

There is plenty of contrast in this poor book, if that be any virtue. Let us turn our eyes away from those scenes of love and cheerfulness, of benevolence and peace. Let us leave Maria in her nursery, hearing the little ones their lessons; and Henry cutting the leaves of a nice new book, fresh from the press, while his home-taught son and heir is playing at pot-hooks and hangers in a copy-book beside him. Let us recollect their purity of mind, their holiness of motive, and their happiness of life; these are the victims of false-witness. And how fares the wretch that would have starved them?

The fate of John Dillaway is at once so tragical, so interesting, and so instructive, that it will be well for us to be transported for awhile, and give this rogue the benefit of honest company.

For many months I had seen a sullen lowering fellow, with cropped head, ironed-legs, and the motley garments of disgrace, driven forth at early morning with his gang of bad compeers; a slave, toiling till night-fall in piling cannon-balls, and chipping off the rust with heavy hammers; a sentinel stood near with a loaded musket; they might not speak to each other, that miserable gang; hope was dead among them; life had no delights; they wreaked their silent hatred on those hammered cannon-balls. The man who struck the fiercest, that sullen convict with the lowering brow, was our stock-jobber, John Dillaway.

Soon after that foretaste of slavery at Woolwich, the ship sailed, freighted with incarnate crime; her captain was a ruffian; (could he help it with such cargoes?) her crew, the offscouring of all nations; and the Chesapeake herself was an old rotten hull, condemned, after one more voyage, to be broken up; a creaking, foul, unsafe vessel, full of rats, cockroaches, and other vermin.

The sun glared ungenially at that blot upon the waters, breeding infectious disease; the waves flung the hated burden from one to the other, disdainful of her freight of sin; the winds had no commission for fair sailing, but whistled through the rigging crossways, howling in the ears of many in that ship, as if they carried ghosts along with them: the very rocks and reefs butted her off the creamy line of breakers, as sea-unicorns distorting; no affectionate farewell blessed her departure; no hearty welcomes await her at the port.

And they sailed many days as in a floating hell, hot, miserable, and cursing; the scanty meal was flung to them like dog's-meat, and they lapped the putrid water from a pail; gang by gang for an hour they might pace the smoking deck, and then and thence were driven down to fester in the hold for three-and-twenty more. O, those closed hatches by night! what torments were the kernel of that ship! Suffocated by the heat and noxious smells; bruised against each other, and by each other's blows, as the black unwieldy vessel staggered about among the billows, the wretched mass of human misery wore away those tropical nights in horrid imprecation; worse than crowded slaves upon the Spanish

Main, from the blister of crime upon their souls, and their utter lack of hopefulness for ever.

And now, after all the shattering storms, and haggard sufferings, and degrading terrors of that voyage, they neared the metropolis of sin; some town on Botany Bay, a blighted shore—where each man, looking at his neighbour, sees in him an outcast from heaven. They landed in droves, that ironed flock of men; and the sullenest-looking scoundrel of them all was John Dillaway.

There were murderers among his gang; but human passions, which had hurried them to crime, now had left them as if wrecked upon a lee shore—humbled and remorseful, and heaven's happier sun shed some light upon their faces: there were burglars; but the courage which could dare those deeds, now lending strength to bear the stroke of punishment, enabled them to walk forth even cheerily to meet their doom of labour: there was rape; but he hid himself, ashamed, vowing better things: fiery arson, too, was there, sorry for his rash revenge: also, conspiracy and rebellion, confessing that ambition such as theirs had been wickedness and folly; and common frauds, and crimes, and social sins; bad enough, God wot, yet hopeful; but the mean, heartless, devilish criminality of our young Dagon beat them all. If to be hard-hearted were a virtue, the best man there was Dillaway.

And now they were to be billeted off among the sturdy colonists as farm-servants, near a-kin to slaves; tools in the rough hands of men who pioneer civilization, with all the vices of the social, and all the passions of the savage. And on the strand, where those task-masters congregated to inspect the new-come droves, each man selected according to his mind: the rougher took the roughest, and the gentler, the gentlest; the merry-looking field farmer sought out the cheerful, and the sullen backwoods settler chose the sullen.

Dillaway's master was a swarthy, beetled-browed caitiff, who had worn out his own seven years of penalty, and had now set up tyrant for himself.

As a hewer of wood and a drawer of water, in a stagnant little clearing of the forest, our convict toiled continually—continually—like Caliban: all days alike; hewing at the mighty trunk and hacking up the straggling branches; no hope—no help—no respite; and the iron of servile tyranny entered into his very soul. Ay—ay; the culprit convicted, when he hears in open court, with an impudent assurance, the punishment that awaits him on those penal shores, little knows the terrors of that sentence. Months and years—yea, haply to gray hairs and death, slavery unmitigated—uncomforted; toil and pain; toil and sorrow; toil, and nothing to cheer; even to the end, vain tasked toil. Old hopes, old recollections, old feelings, violently torn up by the roots. No familiar face in sickness, no patient nurse beside the dying bed: no hope for earth, and no prospect of heaven: but, in its varying phases, one gloomy glaring orb of ever-present hell.

It grew intolerable—intolerable; he was beaten, mocked, and almost a maniac. Escape—escape! Oh, blessed thought! into the wild free woods! there, with the birds and flowers, hill and dale, fresh air and liberty! Oh, glad hope—mad hope! His habitual cunning came to his aid; he schemed, he contrived, he accomplished. The jutting heads of the rivets having been diligently rubbed away from his galling fetter by a big stone—a toil of weeks—he one day stood unshackled, having watched his time to be alone. An axe was in his hand, and the saved single dinner of pea-bread. That beetled-browed task-master slumbered in the hut; that brother convict—(why need he care for him, too? every one for himself in this world)—that kinder, humbler, better man was digging in the open; if he wants to escape, let him think of himself: John Dillaway has enough to take care for. Now, then; now, unobserved, unsuspected; now is the chance! Joy, life, and liberty! Oh, glorious prospect—for this inland world is unexplored.

He stole away, with panting heart, and fearfully exulting eye; he ran—ran—ran, for miles—it may have been scores of them—till night-fall, on the soft and pleasant greensward under those high echoing woods. None pursued; safe—safe; and deliciously he slept that night beneath a spreading wattle-tree, after the first sweet meal of freedom.

Next morning, waked up like the starting kangaroos around him (for John Dillaway had not bent the knee in prayer since childhood), off he set triumphant and refreshed: his arm was strong, and he trusted in it, his axe was sharp, and he looked to that for help; he knew no other God. Off he set for miles—miles—miles: still that continuous high acacia wood, though less naturally park-like, often-times choked with briars, and here and there impervious a-head. Was it all this same starving forest to the wide world's end? He dug for roots, and found some acrid bulbs and tubers, which blistered up his mouth; but he was hungry, and ate them; and dreaded as he ate. Were they poisonous? Next to it, Dillaway; so he hurried eagerly to dilute their griping juices with the mountain streams near which he slept: the water was at least kindly cooling to his hot throat; he drank huge draughts, and stayed his stomach.

Next morning, off again: why could he not catch and eat some of those half-tame antelopes? Ha! He lay in wait hours—hours, near the torrent to which they came betimes to slake their thirst: but their beautiful keen eyes saw him askance—and when he rashly hoped to hunt one down afoot, they went like the wind for a minute—then turned to look at him afar off, mockingly—poor, panting, baffled creeper.

No; give it up—this savoury hope of venison; he must go despondently on and on; and he filled his belly with grass. Must he really starve in this interminable wood! He dreamt that night of luxurious city feasts, the turtle, turbot, venison, and champagne; and then how miserably weak he woke. But he must on wearily and lamely, for ever through this wood—objectless, except for life and liberty. Oh, that he could meet some savage, and do him battle for the food he carried; or that a dead bird, or beast, or snake lay upon his path; or that one of those skipping kangaroos would but come within the reach of his oft-aimed hatchet! No: for all the birds and flowers, and the free wild woods, and hill, and dale, and liberty, he was starving—starving; so he browsed the grass as Nebuchadnezzar in his lunacy. And the famished wretch would have gladly been a slave again.

Next morning, he must lie and perish where he slept, or move on: he turned to the left, not to go on for ever; probably, ay, too probably, he had been creeping round a belt. Oh, precious thought of change! for within three hours there was light a-head, light beneath the tangled underwood: he struggled through the last cluster of thick bushes, longing for a sight of fertile plain, and open country. Who knows? are there not men dwelling there with flocks and herds, and food and plenty? Yes—yes, and Dillaway will do among them yet. You envious boughs, delay me not! He tore aside the last that hid his view, and found that he was standing on the edge of an ocean of sand—hot yellow sand to the horizon!

He fainted—he had like to have died; but as for prayer—he only muttered curses on this bitter, famishing disappointment. He dared not strike into the wood again—he dared not advance upon that yellow sea exhausted and unprovisioned: it was his wisdom to skirt the wood; and so he trampled along weakly—weakly. This liberty to starve is horrible!

Is it, John Dillaway? What, have you no compunctions at that word starve? no bitter, dreadful recollections? Remember poor Maria, that own most loving sister, wanting bread through you. Remember Henry Clements, and their pining babe; remember your own sensual feastings and fraudulent exultation, and how you would utterly have starved the good, the kind, the honest! This same bitter cup is filled for your own lips, and you must drink it to the dregs. Have you no compunctions, man? nothing tapping at your heart? for you must *starve*!

No! not yet—not yet! for chance (what Dillaway lyingly called chance)—in his moments of remorse at these reflections, when God had hoped him penitent at last, and, if he still continued so, might save him—sent help in the desert! For, as he reelingly trampled along on the rank herbage between this forest and that sea of sand, just as he was dying of exhaustion, his faint foot trod upon a store of life and health! It was an Emeu's ill-protected nest; and he crushed, where he had trodden, one of those invigorating eggs. Oh, joy—joy—no thanks—but sensual joy! There were three of them, and each one meat for a day; ash-coloured without, but the within—the within—full of sweet and precious yolk! Oh, rich feast, luscious and refreshing: cheer up—cheer up: keep one to cross the desert with: ay—ay, luck will come at last to clever Jack! how shrewd it was of me to find those eggs!

Thus do the wicked forget thee, blessed God! thou hast watched this bad man day by day, and all the dark nights through, in tender expectation of some good: Thou hast been with him hourly in that famishing forest, tempting him by starvation to—repentance; and how gladly did Thine eager mercy seize this first opportunity of half-formed penitence to bless and help him—even him, liberally and unasked! Thanks to Thee—thanks to Thee! Why did not that man thank Thee? Who more grieved at his thanklessness than Thou art? Who more sorry for the righteous and necessary doom which the impenitence of heartlessness drags down upon itself?

And Providence was yet more kind, and man yet more ungrateful; mercy abounding over the abundant sin. For the famished vagrant diligently sought about for more rich prizes; and, as the manner is of those unnatural birds to leave their eggs carelessly to the hatching of the sunshine, he soon stumbled on another nest. "Ha—ha!" said he, "clever Jack Dillaway of Broker's alley isn't done up yet: no—no, trust him for taking care of number one; now then for the desert; with these four huge eggs and my trusty hatchet, deuce take it, but I'll manage somehow!"

Thus, deriving comfort from his bold hard heart, he launched unhesitatingly upon that sea of sand: with aching toil through the loose hot soil he ploughed his weary way, footsore, for leagues—leagues—lengthened leagues; yellow sand all round, before, and on either hand, as far as eye can stretch, and behind and already in the distance that terrible forest of starvation. But what, then, is the name of this burnt plain, unwatered by one liquid drop, unvisited even by dews in the cold dry night? Have you not yet found a heart, man, to thank Heaven for that kind supply of recreative nourishment, sweet as infant's food, the rich delicious yolk, which bears up still your halting steps across this world of sand? No heart— no heart of flesh—but a stone—a cold stone, and hard as yonder rocky hillock.

He climbed it for a view—and what a view! a panorama of perfect desolation, a continent of vegetable death. His spirit almost failed within him; but he must on—on, or perish where he stood. Taking no count of time, and heedless as to whither he might wander, so it be not back again along that awful track of liberty he longed for, he crept on by little and little, often resting, often dropping for fatigue, night and day —day and night: he had made his last meal; he laid him down to die—and already the premonitory falcon flapped him with its heavy wing. Ha! what are all those carrion fowls congregated there for? Are they battening on some dead carcase? O, hope—hope! there is the smell of food upon the wind: up, man, up—battle with those birds, drive them away, hew down that fierce white eagle with your axe; what right have they to precious food, when man, their monarch, starves? So, the poor emaciated culprit seized their putrid prey, and the scared fowls hovered but a little space above, waiting instinctively for this new victim: they had not left him much—it was a feast of remnants—pickings from the skeleton of some small creature that had perished in the desert—a wombat, probably, starved upon its travels; but a royal feast it was to that famishing wretch: and, gathering up the remainder of those priceless morsels, which he saved for some more fearful future, again he crept upon his way. Still the same, night and day—day and night—for he could only travel a league a-day: and at length, a shadowy line between the sand and sky—far, far off, but circling the horizon as a bow of hope. Shall it be a land of plenty, green, well-watered meadows, the pleasant homes of man, though savage, not unfriendly? O hope, unutterable! or is it (O despair!) another of those dreadful woods, starving solitude under the high-arched gum-trees.

Onward he crept; and the line on the horizon grew broader and darker: onward, still; he was exulting, he had conquered, he was bold and hard as ever. He got nearer, now within some dozen miles; it was an indistinct distance, but green at any rate; huzza—never mind night-fall; he cannot wait, nor rest, with this Elysium before him: so he toiled along through all the black night, and a friendly storm of rain refreshed him, as his thirsty pores drank in the cooling stream. Aha! by morning's dawn he should be standing on the edge of that green paradise, fresh as a young lion, and no thanks to any one but his own shrewd indomitable self.

Morning dawned—and through the vague twilight loomed some high and tangled wall of green foliage, stretching seemingly across the very world. Most sickening sight! a matted, thorny jungle, one of those primeval woods again, but closer, thicker, darker than the park-like one before; rank and prickly herbage in a rotting swamp, crowding up about the stately trees. Must he battle his way through? Well, then, if it must be so, he must and will; any thing rather than this hot and blistering sand. If he is doomed by fate to starve, be it in the shade, not in that fierce sun. So, he weakly plied his hatchet, flinging himself with boldness on that league-thick hedge of thorns; his way was choked with thorns; he struggled under tearing spines, and through prickly underwood, and over tangled masses of briery plants, clinging to him every where around, as with a thousand taloned claws; he is exhausted, extrication is impossible; he beats the tough creepers with his dulled hatchet, as a wounded man vainly; ha! one effort more—a dying effort—must he be impaled upon these sharp aloes, and strange-leafed prickly shrubs; they have caught him there, those thirsty poisoned hooks, innumerable as his sins; his way, whichever way he looks, is hedged up high with thorns—thick-set thorns—sturdy, tearing thorns, that he cannot battle through them. Emaciated, bleeding, rent, fainting, famished, he must perish in the merciless thicket into which hard-heartedness had flung him!

Before he was well dead, those flapping carrion fowls had found him out; they were famishing too, and half forgot their natural distaste for living meat. He fought them vainly, as the dying fight; soon there were other screams in that echoing solitude, besides the screeching falcons! and when they reached his heart (if its matter aptly typified its spirit), that heart should have been a very stone for hardness.

So let the selfish die! alone, in the waste howling wilderness; so let him starve uncared-for, whose boast it was that he had never felt for other than himself—who mocked God, and scorned man—whose motto throughout life, one sensual, unsympathizing, harsh routine, was this: "Take care of the belly, and the heart will take care of itself!"—who never had a wish for other's good, a care for other's evil, a thought beyond his own base carcase; who was a man—no man—a wretch, without a heart. So let him perish miserably; and the white eagles pick his skeleton clean in yonder tangled jungle!

CHAPTER XIX

WHEREIN MATTERS ARE CONCLUDED

Certain folks at Ballyriggan, near Belfast, observe to me, with not a little Irish truth, that it is by no means easy to conclude a history never intended to be finished. It so happens that my good friends the clan Clements are still enjoying life and all it sweets, beneficent in their generation; and as for their hearts' affections, that story without an end will still be heard, ringing on its happy changes, in the presence of God and of his immortal train, when every reader of these records shall have been to this world dead. Out of the heart are the issues of life, and within, it is life's well-spring. Death is but a little narrow gate, in a dark rough pass among the mountains, where each must go alone, one by one, in solemn silence, for the avalanches hanging overhead; one by one, in breathless caution, for there is but barely a footing; one by one, for none can help his brother on the track: the steady eye of faith, the firm foot of righteousness, the staff of hope to comfort and support—these be the only helps. And each one carries with him, as his sole possession on that lonely journey, no heaps of wealth—no trappings of honour; these burdens of the camel must all be lifted off, ere he can struggle through that gully in the rocks—"The Needle's Eye;" but the sole possession which every wayfarer must take with him into those broad plains where only Spirit can be seen, and Sin no longer can be hid, is the shrine of his affections, the casket of his precious pearls in life—his Heart, unmantled and unmasked. And if in time it had been a well of love, flowing towards God in penitence, and irrigating this world's garden with charities and blessed works, that little sparkling stream shall then burst forth from this rocky portal of the grave, a river of joy and peace, to gladden even more the sunny provinces of heaven. For the heart with its affections, never dieth: they may, indeed, flow inward, and corrupt to selfishness; becoming then, in lieu of fountains of waters, gushing forth to everlasting life, a bottomless volcano of hot lava, tempestuous and involved, setting up the creature as his own foul god, and living the perpetual death-bed of the damned; or they may nobly burst the banks of self, and, rising momentarily higher and higher, till every Nilometer is drowned, will seek for ever, with expanding strength, to reach the unapproachable level of that source in the Most Highest whence they originally sprung. For this cause, the kindest fatherly word which ever reached man's ear, the surest scheme for happiness that ever touched his reason, was one from God's own heart—"My son, give me thy heart."

They lived upon the blessing of that Word, our noble, kindly pair. To enlarge upon the thought as respects a better world is well for those who will: for if He that made the eye and framed the ear, by the stronger argument Himself must see and hear, so he that fashioned loveliness and moulded the affections, how well-deserving must that Beautiful Spirit be of his rational creature's heart! Away with mawkish cant and stale sentimentalities! let us think, and speak, and feel as men, framed by nature's urgent law to the lovely and to hate the vile. Oh, that the advocates for Him, the Good One, would oftener plead His cause by the human affections—by generosity, by sympathy, by gentleness and patience, by

Martin Farquhar Tupper

self-denying love, and soul absolving beauty; for these are of the essence of God, and their spiritual influence on reason. A child writes upon his heart that warmer code of morals, which the iron tool of threatening availeth not to grave upon the rock, while the voice of love can change that rock into a spring of water.

But we must descend from our altitudes, and speak of lower things; for the time and space forbid much longer intrusion on your courtesy. A few ravelling threads of this our desultory tale have yet to be gathered up, as tidily as may be. Suffer, then, such mingling of my thoughts: the web I weave has many threads, woven with divers colours. Human nature is nothing if not inconsistent; and I have no more notion of irreverence in turning from a high topic to a low one, than a bee may be fancied to have of irrelevant idleness in flitting from the sweet violet to the scented dahlia. We may gather honey out of every flower. Have you not often noticed, that riches generally come to a man, when he least stands in need of them? Directly a middle-aged heir succeeds to his long-expected heritage, half-a-dozen aunts and second cousins are sure to die off and leave him super-abounding legacies, any one of which would have helped his poverty stricken youth, and made him of independent mind throughout his servile manhood. The other day (the idea remains the same, though the fact is to be questioned) the richest lord in Europe dug up a chest of hoarded coins, many thousand pound's worth, simply because he didn't want it: and, if such particul-arization were not improper or invidious, you or I might name a brace of friends a-piece, who, having once lacked bread in the career of life, suddenly have found themselves monopolizing two or three great fortunes. As too few things are certain, novel writers less like truth in their descriptions, than where ample wealth falls upon the hero just in the nick of time. Providence intends to teach by penury: yes, and by prosperity too: and we almost never see the reward given, or the no less reward withheld, just as the scholar has begun to spell his lesson, and before he has had the chance of getting it by heart.

That another death should occur, in the progress of this tale, must be counted for no fault of mine; especially as I am not about to introduce another death-bed. One need not have the mummy always at our feasts. Surely, too, these deaths have ever been on fit occasion: one broken heart; one bereaved, yet comforted; and one which perished in its sin of uttermost hard-heartedness. And here, if any insurance clerk, or other interested person, will show cause why Mrs. Jane Mackenzie should not die at the age of ninety-two, I would keep her alive if I could; but the fact is, I cannot: she died. Henry Clements never saw her, any more that I, nor dear Maria. But that was no earthly reason wherefore—

First, Maria should not bewail the dear old relative's loss with all her heart and eyes, and children and household in mourning.

Nor, *secondly*, wherefore Mrs. Jane Mackenzie, aforesaid, of Ballyriggan, province of Ulster, should not leave her estate of Ballyriggan, aforesaid, and a vast heap of other property, to the only surviving though distant scion of her family, Henry Clements.

Nor, *thirdly*, wherefore I should not record the fact, as duly bound in my capacity of honest historian.

This accession of property was large, almost overwhelming, when added to Maria's patrimony of three thousand a-year, the produce of St. Benet's Sherehog: for besides and beyond a considerable breadth of Irish acres, sundry houses in Belfast, and an accumulation of half-forgotten funds, the Bank of England found itself necessitated (from particular circumstances of ill-caution in its servants) to refund the whole of that twelve thousand forty-three pounds bank annuities, which Jack Dillaway and his ladies had already made away with.

Rich, however, as Clements had become, he felt himself only as a great lord's steward to help a needy world; and I never heard that he spent a sixpence more upon himself, his equipage, or his family, from being some thousands a-year richer: though I certainly did hear that, owing to this legacy, every tenant upon Ballyriggan, and a vast number of struggling families in Spitalfields and round about St. Benet's, had ample cause to bless Heaven and the good man of Finsbury square. As for dear Maria, it rejoiced her generous heart to find that Henry (whose gentlemanly pride had all along been reproaching him for pauperism) was now become pretty well her equal in wealth; even as her humility long had known him her superior in mind, good looks, and good family.

Another thread in my discourse, hanging loosely on the world, concerns our lady-legatees. What became of Miss Julia, after the safe and successful issue of that vengeful trial, I never heard: and, perhaps, it may be wise not to inquire: if she changed her name, she did not change her nature: and is probably still to be numbered among the sect of Strand peripatetics.

But of Anna Bates I have pleasanter news to tell. With respect to repentance, let us be charitable, and hope, even if we cannot be so sanguine as firmly to believe; but at any rate we may rest assured of an outward reformation, and an honest manner of life. The miracle happened thus: After the trial and condemnation of Dillaway, poor Anna Bates felt entirely disappointed that she had not the chance of better things presented to her mind by transportation; the two approvers, to her dismay—poor thing!—were graciously pardoned for their evidence; and, whereas, the one of them returned to her old courses more devotedly than ever, the other resolved to make one strong effort to extricate her loathing self from the gulf in which she lay. Fortunately for her, our Maria had the heart to pity and to help a frail and fallen sister; and when the poor disconsolate woman, finding her to be the sister of that evil paramour, came to Mrs. Clements in distress, revealing all her past sins and sorrows, and pleading for some generous hand to lift her out of that miserable state, she did not plead in vain. Maria spurned her not away, nor coldly disbelieved her promise of amendment; but, taking counsel of her husband, she gave the poor woman sufficient means of setting up a milliner's shop at Hull, where, under her paternal name of Stellingburne, our Fleet street lady-legatee still survives, earning a decent livelihood, and little suspected amongst her kindly neighbours of ever having been much worse than a strictly honest woman.

For another thread, if the reader, in his ample curiosity, wishes to be informed how it became possible for me to learn the fate of Dillaway, let him know, that up to the hour of escape, I derived it easily from living witnesses; and thereafter, that certain settlers, having set out to explore the country, found a human skeleton stretched upon a thicket which, from the *débris* of convicts' clothes, and the hatchet stamped with his initials, was easily decided to be that bad man's. It always had struck me, as a remarkable piece of retribution, that whereas John made Austral shares a plea for ruining Henry Clements, a howling Austral wilderness was made the means of starving him. Maria never heard what became of her brother; but still looks for his return some day with affectionate and earnest expectation.

Another little matter to be mentioned is the fact, that Henry Clements, in his leisure from business, and freedom from care, resolved to attain some literary glories; and first, he published his now-renowned tragedy of '*Boadicea*,' with his name at length, giving a mint of proceeds to that very proper charity the Theatrical Fund. Secondly, he followed up his tragic triumph by a splendid '*Caractacus*,' by way of a companion picture. Thirdly, he turned to his maligned law-treatise on *Defence*, and boldly published a capital vindication thereof, flinging down his gauntlet to the judges both of law and literature. It was strange, by the way, and instructive also, to find with what a deferential air the wealthy writer now was listened to; and how meekly both '*Watchman*' and '*Corinthian*' kissed the smiling hand of the literary genius, who—gave such sumptuous dinners; for Henry, of his mere kindness, (not bribery—don't imagine him so weak,) now that he was known as a Mæcenas amongst authors, made no invidious distinctions between literary magnates, but effectually overcame evil with good by his hearty hospitality to '*Corinthian*' and '*Watchman*' editors, as well as to other potent wielders of the pen of fame, who had erst-while favoured the productions of his genius.

The last dinner he gave, I, an old friend of the family, was present; and when the ladies went up-stairs, I had, as usual, the honour of enacting vice. It was according to Finsbury taste and custom, to produce toasts and speeches; whether cold high-breeding would have sanctioned this or not, little matters: it was warm and cordial, and we all liked it; moreover, finding ourselves at Rome, we unanimously did as other Romans do: and this I take to be politeness. Among the speeches, that which proposed the health of the host and hostess caused the chiefest roar of clamorous joy: it was a happy-looking friend who spoke, and what he said was much as follows:

"Clements, my dear fellow, you are the happiest man I know—except myself; at least, in one thing I am happier— for I can call you friend, whereas you can only return the compliment with such a sorry substitute as I am."

[This ingenious flattery was much ridiculed afterwards; but I pledge my word the man intended what he said; moreover, he went on, utterly regardless of surrounding critics, in all the seeming egotism of a warm and open heart.]

"Clements—I cannot help telling you how heartily I love you;" (Hear, hear!) "and I wish I had known you thirty years instead of three, to have said so with the unction of my earliest recollections: but we cannot help antiquity, you know. Let us all the rather make up now by heartiness for all lost time. I think, nay, am sure, that I speak the language of all present in telling you I love you:" (an enormous hear-hearing, which rose above the drawing-room floor; Harry Clements singularly distinguished himself, in proving how he loved his father; a fine young fellow he grows too, and I wish, between ourselves, to catch him for a son-in-law some day;)—"Yes, Clements, I do love you, and your children, and your wife, for there is the charm of heart about you all: in yourself, in your Maria, in that fine frank youth, and those dear warm girls up stairs" (every word was bravoed to the echo), "in every one of you, all the charities and amenities, all the kindnesses and the cheerfulness of life appear to be embodied; you love both God and man; the rich and the poor alike may bless you, Clements, and your admirable Maria; whilst, as for yourselves, you may both well thank God, whose mercy made you what you are."

Clements hid his face, and Harry sobbed with joyfulness.

"Friends! a toast and sentiment, with all the honours: 'This happy family! and may all who know them now, or come to hear of them in future, cultivate as they do all the home affections, and acknowledge that there is no wealth of man's, which may compare with riches of the heart.'"

Martin Farquhar Tupper

Choose from Thousands of 1stWorldLibrary Classics By

A. M. Barnard
Ada Leverson
Adolphus William Ward
Aesop
Agatha Christie
Alexander Aaronsohn
Alexander Kielland
Alexandre Dumas
Alfred Gatty
Alfred Ollivant
Alice Duer Miller
Alice Turner Curtis
Alice Dunbar
Allen Chapman
Alleyne Ireland
Ambrose Bierce
Amelia E. Barr
Amory H. Bradford
Andrew Lang
Andrew McFarland Davis
Andy Adams
Angela Brazil
Anna Alice Chapin
Anna Sewell
Annie Besant
Annie Hamilton Donnell
Annie Payson Call
Annie Roe Carr
Annonaymous
Anton Chekhov
Archibald Lee Fletcher
Arnold Bennett
Arthur C. Benson
Arthur Conan Doyle
Arthur M. Winfield
Arthur Ransome
Arthur Schnitzler
Arthur Train
Atticus
B.H. Baden-Powell
B. M. Bower
B. C. Chatterjee
Baroness Emmuska Orczy
Baroness Orczy
Basil King
Bayard Taylor
Ben Macomber
Bertha Muzzy Bower
Bjornstjerne Bjornson

Booth Tarkington
Boyd Cable
Bram Stoker
C. Collodi
C. E. Orr
C. M. Ingleby
Carolyn Wells
Catherine Parr Traill
Charles A. Eastman
Charles Amory Beach
Charles Dickens
Charles Dudley Warner
Charles Farrar Browne
Charles Ives
Charles Kingsley
Charles Klein
Charles Hanson Towne
Charles Lathrop Pack
Charles Romyn Dake
Charles Whibley
Charles Willing Beale
Charlotte M. Braeme
Charlotte M. Yonge
Charlotte Perkins Stetson
Clair W. Hayes
Clarence Day Jr.
Clarence E. Mulford
Clemence Housman
Confucius
Coningsby Dawson
Cornelis DeWitt Wilcox
Cyril Burleigh
D. H. Lawrence
Daniel Defoe
David Garnett
Dinah Craik
Don Carlos Janes
Donald Keyhoe
Dorothy Kilner
Dougan Clark
Douglas Fairbanks
E. Nesbit
E. P. Roe
E. Phillips Oppenheim
E. S. Brooks
Earl Barnes
Edgar Rice Burroughs
Edith Van Dyne
Edith Wharton

Edward Everett Hale
Edward J. O'Biren
Edward S. Ellis
Edwin L. Arnold
Eleanor Atkins
Eleanor Hallowell Abbott
Eliot Gregory
Elizabeth Gaskell
Elizabeth McCracken
Elizabeth Von Arnim
Ellem Key
Emerson Hough
Emilie F. Carlen
Emily Bronte
Emily Dickinson
Enid Bagnold
Enilor Macartney Lane
Erasmus W. Jones
Ernie Howard Pie
Ethel May Dell
Ethel Turner
Ethel Watts Mumford
Eugene Sue
Eugenie Foa
Eugene Wood
Eustace Hale Ball
Evelyn Everett-green
Everard Cotes
F. H. Cheley
F. J. Cross
F. Marion Crawford
Fannie E. Newberry
Federick Austin Ogg
Ferdinand Ossendowski
Fergus Hume
Florence A. Kilpatrick
Fremont B. Deering
Francis Bacon
Francis Darwin
Frances Hodgson Burnett
Frances Parkinson Keyes
Frank Gee Patchin
Frank Harris
Frank Jewett Mather
Frank L. Packard
Frank V. Webster
Frederic Stewart Isham
Frederick Trevor Hill
Frederick Winslow Taylor

Friedrich Kerst
Friedrich Nietzsche
Fyodor Dostoyevsky
G.A. Henty
G.K. Chesterton
Gabrielle E. Jackson
Garrett P. Serviss
Gaston Leroux
George A. Warren
George Ade
Geroge Bernard Shaw
George Cary Eggleston
George Durston
George Ebers
George Eliot
George Gissing
George MacDonald
George Meredith
George Orwell
George Sylvester Viereck
George Tucker
George W. Cable
George Wharton James
Gertrude Atherton
Gordon Casserly
Grace E. King
Grace Gallatin
Grace Greenwood
Grant Allen
Guillermo A. Sherwell
Gulielma Zollinger
Gustav Flaubert
H. A. Cody
H. B. Irving
H.C. Bailey
H. G. Wells
H. H. Munro
H. Irving Hancock
H. R. Naylor
H. Rider Haggard
H. W. C. Davis
Haldeman Julius
Hall Caine
Hamilton Wright Mabie
Hans Christian Andersen
Harold Avery
Harold McGrath
Harriet Beecher Stowe
Harry Castlemon
Harry Coghill
Harry Houidini

Hayden Carruth
Helent Hunt Jackson
Helen Nicolay
Hendrik Conscience
Hendy David Thoreau
Henri Barbusse
Henrik Ibsen
Henry Adams
Henry Ford
Henry Frost
Henry James
Henry Jones Ford
Henry Seton Merriman
Henry W Longfellow
Herbert A. Giles
Herbert Carter
Herbert N. Casson
Herman Hesse
Hildegard G. Frey
Homer
Honore De Balzac
Horace B. Day
Horace Walpole
Horatio Alger Jr.
Howard Pyle
Howard R. Garis
Hugh Lofting
Hugh Walpole
Humphry Ward
Ian Maclaren
Inez Haynes Gillmore
Irving Bacheller
Isabel Cecilia Williams
Isabel Hornibrook
Israel Abrahams
Ivan Turgenev
J.G.Austin
J. Henri Fabre
J. M. Barrie
J. M. Walsh
J. Macdonald Oxley
J. R. Miller
J. S. Fletcher
J. S. Knowles
J. Storer Clouston
J. W. Duffield
Jack London
Jacob Abbott
James Allen
James Andrews
James Baldwin

James Branch Cabell
James DeMille
James Joyce
James Lane Allen
James Lane Allen
James Oliver Curwood
James Oppenheim
James Otis
James R. Driscoll
Jane Abbott
Jane Austen
Jane L. Stewart
Janet Aldridge
Jens Peter Jacobsen
Jerome K. Jerome
Jessie Graham Flower
John Buchan
John Burroughs
John Cournos
John F. Kennedy
John Gay
John Glasworthy
John Habberton
John Joy Bell
John Kendrick Bangs
John Milton
John Philip Sousa
John Taintor Foote
Jonas Lauritz Idemil Lie
Jonathan Swift
Joseph A. Altsheler
Joseph Carey
Joseph Conrad
Joseph E. Badger Jr
Joseph Hergesheimer
Joseph Jacobs
Jules Vernes
Julian Hawthrone
Julie A Lippmann
Justin Huntly McCarthy
Kakuzo Okakura
Karle Wilson Baker
Kate Chopin
Kenneth Grahame
Kenneth McGaffey
Kate Langley Bosher
Kate Langley Bosher
Katherine Cecil Thurston
Katherine Stokes
L. A. Abbot
L. T. Meade

L. Frank Baum
Latta Griswold
Laura Dent Crane
Laura Lee Hope
Laurence Housman
Lawrence Beasley
Leo Tolstoy
Leonid Andreyev
Lewis Carroll
Lewis Sperry Chafer
Lilian Bell
Lloyd Osbourne
Louis Hughes
Louis Joseph Vance
Louis Tracy
Louisa May Alcott
Lucy Fitch Perkins
Lucy Maud Montgomery
Luther Benson
Lydia Miller Middleton
Lyndon Orr
M. Corvus
M. H. Adams
Margaret E. Sangster
Margret Howth
Margaret Vandercook
Margaret W. Hungerford
Margret Penrose
Maria Edgeworth
Maria Thompson Daviess
Mariano Azuela
Marion Polk Angellotti
Mark Overton
Mark Twain
Mary Austin
Mary Catherine Crowley
Mary Cole
Mary Hastings Bradley
Mary Roberts Rinehart
Mary Rowlandson
M. Wollstonecraft Shelley
Maud Lindsay
Max Beerbohm
Myra Kelly
Nathaniel Hawthrone
Nicolo Machiavelli
O. F. Walton
Oscar Wilde

Owen Johnson
P.G. Wodehouse
Paul and Mabel Thorne
Paul G. Tomlinson
Paul Severing
Percy Brebner
Percy Keese Fitzhugh
Peter B. Kyne
Plato
Quincy Allen
R. Derby Holmes
R. L. Stevenson
R. S. Ball
Rabindranath Tagore
Rahul Alvares
Ralph Bonehill
Ralph Henry Barbour
Ralph Victor
Ralph Waldo Emmerson
Rene Descartes
Ray Cummings
Rex Beach
Rex E. Beach
Richard Harding Davis
Richard Jefferies
Richard Le Gallienne
Robert Barr
Robert Frost
Robert Gordon Anderson
Robert L. Drake
Robert Lansing
Robert Lynd
Robert Michael Ballantyne
Robert W. Chambers
Rosa Nouchette Carey
Rudyard Kipling
Saint Augustine
Samuel B. Allison
Samuel Hopkins Adams
Sarah Bernhardt
Sarah C. Hallowell
Selma Lagerlof
Sherwood Anderson
Sigmund Freud
Standish O'Grady
Stanley Weyman
Stella Benson
Stella M. Francis

Stephen Crane
Stewart Edward White
Stijn Streuvels
Swami Abhedananda
Swami Parmananda
T. S. Ackland
T. S. Arthur
The Princess Der Ling
Thomas A. Janvier
Thomas A Kempis
Thomas Anderton
Thomas Bailey Aldrich
Thomas Bulfinch
Thomas De Quincey
Thomas Dixon
Thomas H. Huxley
Thomas Hardy
Thomas More
Thornton W. Burgess
U. S. Grant
Upton Sinclair
Valentine Williams
Various Authors
Vaughan Kester
Victor Appleton
Victor G. Durham
Victoria Cross
Virginia Woolf
Wadsworth Camp
Walter Camp
Walter Scott
Washington Irving
Wilbur Lawton
Wilkie Collins
Willa Cather
Willard F. Baker
William Dean Howells
William le Queux
W. Makepeace Thackeray
William W. Walter
William Shakespeare
Winston Churchill
Yei Theodora Ozaki
Yogi Ramacharaka
Young E. Allison
Zane Grey

www.ingramcontent.com/pod-product-compliance
Lightning Source LLC
Chambersburg PA
CBHW031835170626
46807CB00004B/1477